THE IMPORTANCE OF

Galileo Galilei

by Deborah Hitzeroth and Sharon Heerboth

Lucent Books, P.O. Box 289011, San Diego, CA 92198-9011

These and other titles are included in The Importance Of biography series:

Benjamin Franklin
Chief Joseph
Christopher Columbus
Marie Curie
Galileo Galilei
Richard M. Nixon
Jackie Robinson
H.G. Wells

Library of Congress Cataloging-in-Publication Data

Hitzeroth, Deborah, 1961–
    Galileo Galilei / by Deborah Hitzeroth and Sharon Heerboth.
        p.   cm.—(The Importance of)
    Includes bibliographical references and index.
    Summary: A biography of mathematician, physicist, and astron-omer Galileo, from his early years to his confrontations with the church, his last years, and his legacy.
    ISBN 1-56006-027-1:
    1. Galilei, Galileo, 1564–1642—Juvenile literature.   2. Astron-omers—Italy—Biography—Juvenile literature. [1. Galileo, 1564–1642. 2. Scientists.]
I. Heerboth, Sharon, 1959–   . II. Title.   III. Series.
QB36.G2H54   1992
520'.92—dc20   92-25957
[B]   CIP
                                                                  AC

Printed in the U.S.A.

Contents

Foreword

THE IMPORTANCE OF biography series deals with individuals who have made a unique contribution to history. The editors of the series have deliberately chosen to cast a wide net and include people from all fields of endeavor. Individuals from politics, music, art, literature, philosophy, science, sports, and religion are all represented. In addition, the editors did not restrict the series to individuals whose accomplishments have helped change the course of history. Of necessity, this criterion would have eliminated many whose contribution was great, though limited. Charles Darwin, for example, was responsible for radically altering the scientific view of the natural history of the world. His achievements continue to impact the study of science today. Others, such as Chief Joseph of the Nez Percé, played a pivotal role in the history of their own people. While Joseph's influence does not extend much beyond the Nez Percé, his nonviolent resistance to white expansion and his continuing role in protecting his tribe and his homeland remain an inspiration to all.

These biographies are more than factual chronicles. Each volume attempts to emphasize an individual's contributions both in his or her own time and for posterity. For example, the voyages of Christopher Columbus opened the way to European colonization of the New World. Unquestionably, his encounter with the New World brought monumental changes to both Europe and the Americas in his day. Today, however, the broader impact of Columbus's voyages is being critically scrutinized. *Christopher Columbus,* as well as every biography in The Importance Of series, includes and evaluates the most recent scholarship available on each subject.

Each author includes a wide variety of primary and secondary source quotations to document and substantiate his or her work. All quotes are footnoted to show readers exactly how and where biographers derive their information, as well as provide stepping stones to further research. These quotations enliven the text by giving readers eyewitness views of the life and times of each individual covered in The Importance Of series.

Finally, each volume is enhanced by photographs, bibliographies, chronologies, and comprehensive indexes. For both the casual reader and the student engaged in research, The Importance Of biographies will be a fascinating adventure into the lives of people who have helped shape humanity's past, present, and will continue to shape its future.

Important Dates in the Life of Galileo Galilei

Galileo is born in Pisa.	**1564**	Family moves to Florence; Galileo receives first formal education.
Student at University of Pisa.	**1574**	
	1581	
	1585	Returns to Florence; Galileo leaves university without degree.
Professor of mathematics at Pisa; while there writes *On Motion;* leaves university as soon as his contract is finished.	**1589**	
	1592	Professor of mathematics at Padua.
	1609	Constructs and uses the telescope; makes discoveries that shock and amaze the world; wins international fame.
Returns to Florence as the grand duke's chief mathematician and philosopher.	**1610**	
	1611	
Caccini's sermon against Galileo; other enemies begin speaking out against him publicly.	**1614**	Fearing his enemies are plotting against him, Galileo travels to Rome to win the pope's support for his work.
The Assayer, Galileo's strongest attack against Aristotle, is published; so well received that Galileo believes he can write a book in support of Copernicus.	**1616**	Third visit to Rome; Galileo tries to defend himself against his enemies' accusations.
	1618	
	1632	*Dialogue* is published—Galileo's most famous work, which supports works of Copernicus and ridicules followers of Aristotle; book brings about his downfall.
Galileo tried by the Inquisition; his works are banished, and he is sentenced to house arrest for the remainder of his life.	**1632**	
Galileo dies under house arrest.	**1638**	*Discourses on Two New Sciences* is published—Galileo's final work, which discusses the theories of motion and energy.
	1642	

The Wrangler

In the history of science, Galileo stands out as one of the world's most important figures. As an inventor, scholar, and researcher, he carved out new scientific methods and trod new scientific ground. He was also a revolutionary, a challenger of accepted notions of his day, and a critic of the most powerful people in academia and the Roman Catholic church. In his uncompromising search for the truth, Galileo ushered in the scientific revolution.

Galileo was a pioneer in scientific experimentation and research, and his methods revolutionized the study of science.

In Galileo's time, most scientists and learned people believed that the keys to the universe resided with the thinkers of the past—Greek and Roman philosophers whose works had recently been rediscovered. These works, along with the Bible, made up the sum total of scientific knowledge. When scientists found evidence that seemed to contradict these authorities, they faulted the evidence rather than the authorities.

Galileo opposed many of these time-honored theories with untiring relish. His constant questioning came early, while he was still a student, and earned him the nickname the Wrangler. He was a fiery and impassioned speaker who often attempted to shock people into questioning the theories which they accepted simply because others accepted them.

Galileo's methods of experimentation and observation also changed the scientific world. Galileo was interested in everything in the natural world and believed that the inner workings of the universe could be revealed through patient study and painstaking research.

Unfortunately, Galileo was also a man ahead of his time. By challenging almost everyone, Galileo made enemies of many accepted authorities and, especially, the

Galileo believed the secrets of the universe would be revealed through careful observation.

church. Forced to recant his ideas and to live out the end of his life in isolation, Galileo took the full force of the punishment for being different in a time that demanded conformity. This, perhaps, is what makes Galileo's accomplishments even more astonishing. He refused to compromise his principles, in spite of the severe punishment he would receive. Yet Galileo's sacrifice did not go unnoticed. Today, his theories still influence scientific knowledge, while those of the church that tried to crush him are viewed as hopelessly outdated. *"Eppur si muove,"*—the earth does move—Galileo is rumored to have whispered after his sentencing by the Inquisition, the religious tribunal that judged him. And, indeed, it does.

1 The Early Years

At the time Galileo was born, a revolution of ideas was under way in Italy. The nation was in the midst of the Renaissance, a time of intellectual and artistic awakening, and scientists as well as artists were interested in exploring the natural world around them. The Renaissance, which had begun in Italy in the fourteenth century and spread throughout Europe during the fifteenth century, was a widespread reaction against the Middle Ages. During the Middle Ages, roughly 500–1450, the time between the fall of the Roman Empire and the beginning of the Renaissance, the elaborate

Roman school system had disappeared, and formal education was limited. Most people were uneducated and had little interest in science or scholarship. Even if people were interested in these ideas, few had the time or the opportunity to pursue them. Most were poor, spending their days working long, hard hours to maintain even a meager existence. During the Renaissance, however, all of this was changing. Italian scholars were delving into mechanics and investigating the fields of motion and mathematics. The invention of the printing press enabled them to distribute

The invention of the printing press allowed scholars to distribute their discoveries throughout Europe.

Galileo was born in Pisa, Italy, on February 15, 1564, to a noble family that had fallen on hard times.

their ideas as never before. Scholars were producing pamphlets, booklets, and manuscripts to spread their discoveries around the world.

The Power of the Church

At the same time that the world was experiencing an awakening interest in learning, forces were at work to stop the spread of new ideas, especially in Italy, where the power of the Catholic church was threatened by these new events. During the Middle Ages, the Catholic church had become a powerful force in Europe. As the largest landowner, the church had the power to crown kings, make laws, and control what was taught in schools. Virtually everyone was a member of the Catholic church, and its rituals marked events throughout life— baptizing babies, blessing marriages, and performing funeral rites. Anyone who fought the church could be denied these rites and thus be denied entry into heaven, according to church teaching. The church required unquestioning adherence to its principles and tenets.

The growing interest in art, science, and nature during the Renaissance often clashed with the church's teachings. Religious leaders thought that some scientific ideas contradicted what was written in the Bible. Church leaders were afraid that if people began to question their biblical teachings, the church would lose much of its political and social power.

Family Background

Galileo came of age during this time of political and social change. Born on February 15, 1564, Galileo was the eldest of seven children of the Galilei family, an old and noble Florentine line that had fallen on hard times. His mother, Giulia, was well educated, which was unusual for women in her time. Galileo's father, Vincenzo, was a respected musician and an outspoken and uncompromising man who defended his ideas regardless of whom he challenged or offended. From an early age, Galileo was taught by his father to think for himself and to question authority.

An example of Vincenzo's uncompromising nature was his challenge of accepted music authorities of his day. In the 1500s music theory was based on mathematical rules that every musician strictly followed. The rules were based on complex mathematical ratios inherited from ancient times. It was believed that if musicians departed from these rules, their music would be terrible. Vincenzo thought these rules were outdated and unnecessary. He argued that they were developed at a time when the number of instruments was extremely limited. Better musical instruments with greater ranges had been developed, but music was still written following these very limited guidelines. Vincenzo experimented with his instruments and found that many melodies were better when they broke these established rules. Vincenzo believed musicians should experiment with these new instruments and come up with new music.

Planting the Seeds of Doubt

The traditional idea of music was supported by most musical theorists, including Geoseffo Zarlino, the master of music at St. Mark's Church in Venice. Zarlino was a politically powerful man who was considered the authority on musical theory. Vincenzo, who had once been a student of Zarlino, wrote to his former teacher of his findings. Zarlino refused to listen. Even though his teacher would not support his ideas, Vincenzo was sure he was right. Without considering the political consequences of his actions, Vincenzo decided to publish his findings. In 1581 Vincenzo's book, *Dialogue of Ancient and Modern Music,* was published in Florence.

The music master at St. Mark's Church in Venice (pictured at right) was Geoseffo Zarlino, who refused to listen to Galileo's father's ideas about breaking musical rules.

The title page from Galileo's father's book,
Dialogue of Ancient and Modern Music.

Vincenzo wrote,

It appears to me that they who in proof of any assertion rely simply on the weight of authority, without adducing any argument in support of it, act very absurdly. I, on the contrary, wish to be allowed freely to question and freely to answer you without any sort of adulation, as well becomes those who are in search of the truth.[1]

As scientist Colin Ronan wrote in *Galileo,* "Vincenzo's experimental approach . . . was [the same one] . . . Galileo was later to [use to] attack the problems and arguments that faced him."[2]

From his father, Galileo learned never to accept an idea as true simply because many people believed it. In addition, Vincenzo taught Galileo a love of learning. Even though the family was poor, Vincenzo made sure that Galileo received an education proper for a young nobleman. Galileo was taught by a private tutor until the family moved to Florence in 1574. Then, at the age of ten, he was sent to study at the monastery of Santa Maria Vallombrosa, a school run by Jesuits, a Catholic order that comprised a powerful branch of the church.

Early Schooling

At Vallombrosa Galileo was taught a mixture of ancient Greek and Roman philosophy and church doctrine. The writings of the great Roman and Greek philosophers had just recently been rediscovered, and most learned people during the Renaissance accepted their theories as the most accurate and well-argued of the day. Much of what Galileo was taught about these works came from the writings of St. Thomas Aquinas, a priest and philosopher who lived from 1226 to 1274. During his life Aquinas had studied many of the ancient Greek philosophers and tried to reconcile their theories with Catholic doctrine. In particular, Aquinas was fascinated with the writings of the ancient Greek Aristotle and devoted his life to writing about how Aristotelian philosophy supported the

The Greek philosopher Aristotle was considered the authority on all questions concerning the universe.

wanted his son to study medicine at the University of Pisa. Once there, however, Galileo quickly began to chafe under the school's sharp restrictions. College students were required to spend long hours memorizing and reciting ancient texts. They were not encouraged to question these texts nor to develop new ideas.

Of the ancient thinkers, Galileo mostly studied the writings of Aristotle, Ptolemy, and Galen. On all questions concerning the nature of the universe, Aristotle was considered the authority. Aristotle, who lived from 384 to 322 B.C., wrote a large number of books explaining the universe with such

The earth was the center of the universe, according to Aristotle. He taught that the sun, moon, stars, and other planets revolved around the earth in concentric spheres.

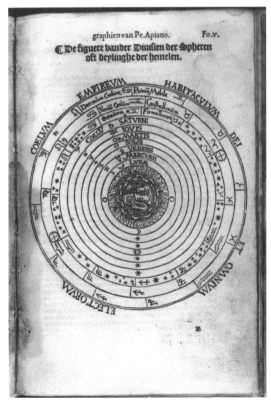

Bible. What Aquinas began, other clergymen continued for more than two hundred years. By 1500, ancient Greek ideas were completely incorporated into Catholic school curriculum.

Galileo left Vallombrosa at the age of seventeen on the advice of his father. Vincenzo

Much of Galileo's early education was based on the writing of St. Thomas Aquinas.

Astronomer Claudius Ptolemy lived in Egypt during the second century.

Galen. Galen had experimented on many animals. But, since human dissection was not practiced in his time, he was not able to verify on humans what he had learned in his experiments with animals. Galen's reliance on animal anatomy led him to make serious mistakes in his theories about human anatomy. Some parts of the human body he described did not exist at all, since they were found only in the anatomy of some animals.

These texts were frustrating to Galileo, because much of what he was forced to read and memorize was in direct contrast

Ptolemy supported Aristotle's view that the earth was the center of the universe, as shown in this diagram.

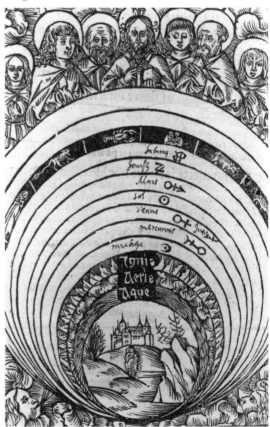

scope and power that for hundreds of years he remained the unchallenged expert on most scientific questions.

Claudius Ptolemy was an astronomer who lived in Alexandria, Egypt, from A.D. 127 to 151. In A.D. 140 Ptolemy published *The Greater Astronomical Syntax,* which supported Aristotle's view of the workings of the universe. Ptolemy believed the sun, moon, and the planets revolved around the earth at regularly spaced distances. He also theorized that the stars hung on the inside of this slowly revolving crystal sphere and that the earth stood in the center of the sphere. Ptolemy believed that outside of this sphere was heaven and that the angels resided there.

The authority in medicine during this time was a second-century physician named to what he observed daily. Galileo and his fellow students were required to practice human dissection. But Galen's authority was so firmly entrenched that no one would question what he had written. In the classes Galileo attended it was standard practice for a professor to read from one of Galen's books while a demonstrator dissected a body for illustration. Facts that differed from what Galen had written were completely ignored. Galileo asked questions so often that he was soon dubbed the Wrangler by his fellow students. Since these questions were greatly discouraged, Galileo was very unpopular with his teachers, who thought he was haughty, rude, and rebellious.

Galileo made his first scientific discovery when he realized that a swinging chandelier took the same amount of time to complete each swing, regardless of the length of the swing.

Galileo was forced to memorize the writings of Galen, the accepted medical authority of the time, even though his observations directly contradicted Galen's views.

Seeing Is Believing

Galileo was bored and frustrated at the university. He wanted to learn things on his own. As his father had taught him, Galileo believed it was important to learn through observation and experimentation. This belief helped him make his first scientific discovery while still a student. In 1582, during a sermon in the university's cathedral, Galileo noticed a huge chandelier swinging back and forth. Being bored by the sermon, Galileo began to time its swings to the beats of his pulse. To his surprise, he found that all of the swings took the same amount of time no matter how large the swing.

Galileo compared the chandelier to a pendulum and wondered if other pendulums, regardless of size, acted the same way. After the service he returned to his room and began to experiment with his idea. Later he wrote of his experiment:

> I took two balls, one of lead and one of cork, the former more than a hundred times heavier than the latter and suspended them by means of two equal fine threads. . . . I let them go at the same instant . . . [and] these free goings and returnings repeated a hundred times showed clearly that the heavy body maintains so nearly the period of the light body that neither in a hundred swings nor even a thousand will the two balls [be out of rhythm] by as much as a single moment, so perfectly do they keep step.[3]

Galileo used his experiments to prove that all pendulums with strings of equal length swing in equal time. This was the first time a scientist had used observation and experimentation to prove a theory. No one knew of Galileo's historic experiment at the time, but with it he began breaking with the Greek authorities and ultimately changing the field of science. Also, unlike other scientists of his time, he was determined to put his theory to practical use. He used what he learned to build an instrument for measuring a person's pulse rate. The instrument, which Galileo called the *pulsilogia,* consisted of a string fastened to a piece of wood with a ball attached to one end. Galileo matched the swing of his pendulum with the pulse of a healthy person and marked the distance of the swing on the wooden board. Doctors could then use the device to compare a sick person's pulse to that marked on the wooden board. The instrument allowed the detection of even the slightest abnormality in a patient's pulse. Galileo's device was a great help to doctors, who quickly started using it, and it was later used by other scientists to build accurate clocks.

A Change of Plans

Shortly after this experiment Galileo decided to stop studying to be a doctor. He wanted to study mathematics and continue his experiments. Galileo knew he would have to leave the school to pursue the field because the university did not have a mathematics teacher. Colleges placed little importance on mathematics and science, and the mathematics teaching position at Pisa had been vacant for a number of years.

In 1583 Galileo finally persuaded his father to let him have a private mathematics tutor. Vincenzo arranged for his son to take lessons from Ostilio Ricci, a family friend who was the tutor to the young noblemen at the court of the grand duke of Florence. During this year the grand duke was staying in Pisa, so Galileo had easy access to Ricci. The decision to study mathematics shaped the rest of Galileo's life and ultimately changed the world.

While studying with Ricci, Galileo read the works of the Greek scientist Archimedes. Archimedes was one of the few ancient scientists who believed in learning through observation and trial. Here, finally, was an authority Galileo could understand and respect. Galileo wrote, "Those who read his works realize only too clearly how inferior are all other minds compared with Archimedes."[4]

In the work of the great Greek mathematician and inventor, Archimedes, Galileo found a soulmate who also believed in experimentation.

His studies with Ricci further convinced Galileo that he was better suited to study science and mathematics rather than medicine. His belief, combined with the teasing of the other students and the hostility of his professors, made Galileo leave Pisa in 1585. He had not attained a degree and returned home to devote himself to mathematics.

Galileo helped support his family by giving private mathematics lessons to local students. He soon gained a local reputation as a mathematics expert. Galileo wanted to make his living teaching mathematics and doing research. That meant teaching at a university, but it was very hard to find a place at a university for a relatively unknown young man who had

not finished his degree. Usually professorships were given to men who had outstanding reputations in their field or who were politically powerful.

Finally, with the help of a powerful friend, Marquis Guidobaldo del Monte of Pesaro, Galileo was able to obtain a teaching position at the University of Pisa in 1589. At the age of twenty-five Galileo returned as an equal to the college where professors thought of him as a troublemaker. Upon his return, he proved to be as radical a teacher as he had been a student.

A Sharp Tongue

Galileo received a cool reception from his new colleagues, and he did nothing to improve this response. Galileo had a sharp wit and little tolerance for people who did not understand his ideas. He began making enemies shortly after he arrived at the university. Galileo ridiculed the faculty by writing and distributing a poem mocking the university's rule that professors had to wear their academic robes at all times. No one was safe from the sting of his wit. He wrote of the ancient poet Tasso that he "besmeared too much paper," which only made "pap for cats." In other words, his work was only good enough to be used for cat litter.

Galileo's approach to teaching also brought criticism. The other professors accused him of conducting his classes like a carnival. While other students learned by memorization, Galileo's students learned by experimentation. For example, when teaching about sound, Galileo had pistols fired from a distance. He then had his students count the seconds between when they saw the flash and when they heard the noise from the pistol. In this way his students learned how sound traveled at a measurable speed.

During this time Galileo found time for writing as well. He wrote a small book entitled *On Motion*. Throughout the book he was merciless in his attack on Aristotle. In one chapter he wrote, "In practically everything he wrote about local motion, he wrote the opposite of truth." Galileo did not publish his book, but circulated it among friends. What he wrote alarmed the university. Some viewed it as a radical document that argued against the current knowledge of physics. Those who supported Aristotle became openly hostile toward the young professor. His enemies began packing the auditorium every time he lectured, to drown out his speech with their hissing and booing.

By the end of his three-year appointment, Galileo had not only failed to win the faculty's support for his ideas but had also gained many powerful enemies. When his contract expired in 1592 Galileo wisely decided to resign his post. He left the university to look for a place where he could freely explore his beliefs.

He returned home dismayed and worried about his future. But his worry quickly turned into excitement when his friends helped him obtain a job as the teacher of mathematics at the University of Padua.

The opportunity came just as Galileo was on the verge of poverty. It had been a year since he left Pisa, and he had been able to earn little income. Galileo was so poor when he received the job in 1592 that he had to walk from Florence to Padua, a distance of a hundred miles. But he arrived in Padua ready to make a fresh start.

Chapter

2 Years of Discovery

Galileo's years at Padua were the happiest and most productive of his life. The school allowed its professors the freedom to explore their own ideas, and Galileo found the environment he needed to make new discoveries.

Galileo published numerous papers and treatises at Padua which gained him a reputation as a brilliant scientist. He wrote papers on the science of machines and on how to construct efficient military buildings and forts. His papers were copied and sent to universities and royal courts all over Europe and began to influence scientists and statesmen.

Galileo was careful to prove his theories with experiments that offered evidence about how and why things happened. He believed that

for each effect there is a prime and true cause. Between cause and effect there exists a firm and constant relation, such that . . . each time that we observe a [change] in the effect there must be a [change] in the cause.[5]

A view of the city of Padua. Galileo made many discoveries during his years teaching here because the school allowed him to explore his own ideas.

Galileo's military compass was used by engineers and soldiers, and became a status symbol among the rich.

In 1597 Galileo invented an instrument that he called the military compass. This instrument was not really a compass, but more a combination divider and slide rule. It was used to solve mathematical and geometrical problems. The invention was quickly picked up and used by engineers to aid in the construction of buildings. Soldiers used it to determine the trajectory (path) of weapons and the height of fortress walls. Owning one of Galileo's compasses quickly became a status symbol among the wealthy. Galileo's invention was ordered by kings, generals, engineers, and teachers in Italy, France, and Germany. People came from all across Europe to Padua to receive instruction in its use. Galileo produced over three hundred of these instruments. This was an amazing number for the time, considering that every part had to be made by hand.

Galileo's life was filled with teaching at the university, tutoring private students, and experimenting in his workshop. Still, he found time to study the works of the ancient authors and compare their findings with what he observed. Often he found contradictions between what he read and what he observed in nature. Increasingly, Galileo became convinced that the ideas of Aristotle and Ptolemy were wrong, especially in the area of astronomy. He read the works of Copernicus and began to believe he had a more accurate picture of the universe.

Nicolaus Copernicus was a Polish doctor, lawyer, clergyman, and amateur astronomer who lived in the early 1500s. After studying the stars for more than twenty years, Copernicus became convinced that the earth was not the center of the universe. Rather, he thought, the earth and planets rotated around the sun. Copernicus published his ideas in 1543 in a book titled *De Revolutionibus Oribum Caelestium (On the Revolution of the Celestial Orbs).* Being a deeply religious man, and fearing the consequences of supporting ideas that were not sanctioned by the church, Copernicus waited until near the

An Opposing View

Polish-born Nicolaus Copernicus developed the theory that the sun is the center of the universe and that all of the planets rotate around the sun. The following is an excerpt from his book De Revolutionibus Oribum Caelestium, *published in 1543.*

"That the Earth is not the centre of all revolutions is proved by the apparently irregular motions of the Planets and the variation in their distances from Earth. These would be unintelligible if they moved in circles [around] the Earth. . . . We shall place the Sun himself at the centre of the Universe. All this is suggested by the systematic procession of events and the harmony of the whole Universe, if only we face the facts, as they say, 'with both eyes open'. . . . We therefore assert that the centre of the Earth, carrying the Moon's path, passes in a great orbit among the other Planets in an annual revolution around the Sun . . . that . . . the Sun is the centre of the Universe; and that whereas the Sun is at rest, any apparent motion of the Sun can be better explained by the motion of the Earth. Yet so great is the Universe that though the distance of the Earth from the Sun is not insignificant . . . it is insignificant compared with the distance of the sphere of the fixed stars."

end of his life to have his book published. Legend has it that he received his first copy of the published work on his deathbed only fifteen minutes before he died.

Some scientists were intrigued by Copernicus's ideas, but church leaders quickly ridiculed him. The Protestant leader Martin Luther called Copernicus

the new astrologer who wants to prove the earth moves and goes round. . . . The fool wants to turn the whole art of astronomy upside down. . . . [but] Holy Scripture tells us, so did Joshua bid the sun stand still and not the earth.[6]

Martin Luther, a Protestant leader, ridiculed Copernicus's view of the universe.

Nicolaus Copernicus was a Polish astronomer who became convinced that the earth was not the center of the universe, but instead it revolved around the sun.

Melanchthon, one of Luther's principal followers, also berated Copernicus, saying:

The eyes are witness that the heavens revolve in the space of twenty-four hours. But certain men, either from the love of novelty, or to make a display of ingenuity, have concluded that the earth moves, and they maintain that neither the (fixed stars) nor the sun revolves. . . . Now it is a [lack] of honesty and decency to assert such notions publicly, and the example is [dangerous]. It is part of a good mind to accept the truth as revealed by God and to [surrender] to it.[7]

Since Copernicus was unable to prove his ideas, no one championed his beliefs after his death. The Catholic church ignored his writings, and they faded into obscurity.

Copernicus's idea that the planets revolved around the sun seemed to make sense to Galileo. Galileo knew, however, that he dare not oppose Aristotle's ideas until he could prove their inaccuracy. By opposing the church without some evidence, Galileo feared he would be accused of heresy.

Even though he could not proclaim his ideas publicly, Galileo could share them privately. On August 4, 1597, he wrote to German astronomer Johannes Kepler to discuss Copernicus. Kepler was a strong supporter of Copernicus's theories and had recently written a book championing his ideas.

Kepler's book sparked a debate in the scientific community. Some scientists believed that Kepler and Copernicus must be right, others steadfastly defended Aristotle and the church-supported idea that the earth was the center of the universe. Kepler, who lived in a Protestant country and was safe from persecution by the Catholic church, was free to publish his ideas without proof.

In his August letter to Kepler, Galileo wrote, "Like you, I accepted the Copernican position several years ago. . . . I would dare to publish my thoughts if there were many like you; but since there are not, I shall (not)."[8]

Kepler sent back an impassioned plea for Galileo to publicly support Copernicus's ideas:

I could only have wished that you, who have so profound an insight, would choose another way. . . . Would it not be much better to pull the wagon to its goal by our joint efforts, now that we have got it under way, and gradually, with powerful voices, to shout down the common herd, which really does

Copernicanism

In a letter dated 1597 to German scientist Johannes Kepler, quoted in Laura Fermi and Gilberto Bernardini's Galileo and the Scientific Revolution, *Galileo admits that he believes Copernicus's theory of the universe.*

"I count myself happy, in the search after truth, to have so great an ally as yourself, and one who is so great a friend of the truth itself. . . . I shall read your book to the end, confident of finding much that is excellent in it. I shall do so with the more pleasure because I have been for many years an adherent of the Copernican system, and it explains to me the causes of many of the appearances of nature which are quite unintelligible on the commonly accepted hypothesis [Aristotle's idea of the earth as the center of the universe]. I have collected many arguments for the purpose of refuting the latter, but I do not venture to bring them to the light of publicity for fear of sharing the fate of our master Copernicus, who, although he has earned immortal fame with some, yet with very many (so great is the number of fools) has become an object of ridicule and scorn."

Johannes Kepler was a strong supporter of Copernicus's views of the universe.

not weigh the arguments very carefully? Thus perhaps by cleverness we may bring it to a knowledge of the truth. . . . Be of good cheer, Galileo, and come out publicly.[9]

But even with Kepler's prompting, Galileo was unwilling to go public with his beliefs.

Star Bright

On October 9, 1604, a new star appeared in the sky and gave Galileo a chance to begin promoting Copernicus's theories. The people of Italy were terrified of the

A Fear of Heresy

In this excerpt from the forward to Nicolaus Copernicus's book De Revolutionibus, *he explains how he fears his ideas will be received.*

"I can reckon easily enough . . . that as soon as certain people learn that in these books of mine which I have written about the revolutions of the spheres of the world I attribute certain motions to the [earth] . . . they will immediately shout to have me and my opinion hooted off the stage. . . . And in order that the unlearned as well as the learned might see that I was not seeking to flee from the judgment of many, I preferred to dedicate these results of my nocturnal study to [the pope] rather than to anyone else."

new star. According to the Catholic church, university scholars, and philosophers, the heavens were supposed to be unchangeable. But night after night this new, bright star blazed in the sky. Astrologers predicted that the new star heralded the end of the world. Others, who supported Aristotle's view of the world, refused to believe what they witnessed every night. These people, called Aristotelians, denounced what everyone saw and claimed that it was not a star, but an illusion. Perhaps, they said, it was simply light from the sun bouncing off the moon.

While people around him argued about the meaning of the new star, Galileo made nightly observations of its height in the sky and whether it moved in respect to the other stars. After watching it for weeks, he gave a series of lectures about the star and what he had observed. The Aristotelians were wrong when they claimed the universe was unchangeable, Galileo declared. This was a new star. (We now

know that Galileo's conclusion was incorrect. The new spot of light in the sky was caused by the violent death of a star, not by the birth of a new one. The violent explosions inside the star gave off a tremendous amount of light. When this happened, the star, which had previously been invisible in the sky, could be viewed by the naked eye.)

Galileo's lectures about the bright new star caused a great scandal within the university. Cesare Cremonini, a professor of philosophy and a leading advocate of Aristotle's ideas at Padua, declared Galileo's arguments nonsense. Aristotelian scientists at other universities rushed to support Cremonini. They published a booklet denouncing Galileo's lectures. If what Galileo said was true, then everything they believed about the universe was false. Galileo responded by helping to write a booklet that ridiculed the Aristotelian professors. This satire was very popular and was reprinted in two editions. While the public liked the book, the professors were not

Jan Lippershey invented the telescope in 1608.

amused. For the first time Galileo had enemies who hated him beyond measure.

Perhaps, if Galileo's observation and discussions of astronomy had been limited to the new star, the other professors would have eventually forgiven him. But a new invention soon appeared that connected Galileo with the Copernican debate for the rest of his life.

A Far Seer

Galileo first heard about the invention from one of his former students, a French nobleman named Jacques Badovere. Badovere wrote to tell his old mathematics teacher about a Dutch scientist who had "constructed a spyglass, by means of which . . . objects, though very distant from the eye of the observer, were seen . . . as if near by."[10] The device he was talking about was the telescope. The instrument had been discovered by accident in 1608 by a

Dutch glassmaker named Jan Lippershey. One day, while polishing eyeglasses, Lippershey held the lenses of two different glasses next to each other and noticed that faraway items appeared much closer. The glassmaker fitted the two lenses inside a tube and mounted the tube in his shop as a novelty to attract customers. Galileo was intrigued by his student's report and set out to build a "far-seeing device" of his own. Later he wrote:

> Upon hearing this news . . . [I] set myself to thinking about the problem. The first night . . . I solved it, and on the following day I constructed the instrument and sent word of this to . . . friends at Venice with whom I had discussed the matter the previous day. Immediately afterwards I applied myself to the construction of another and better one.[11]

Within a week of building his first telescope, Galileo constructed a second, better one. Galileo immediately recognized

Galileo used this telescope to locate the moons of Jupiter and the mountains on earth's moon.

away that, even under full sail, two hours and more went by before they could be seen (with the naked eye).[12]

Galileo's telescopes were a public sensation. Poets wrote songs about them and crowds gathered whenever anyone carried one in public. Noblemen from across Europe wanted to own one of Galileo's far-seeing devices because his were superior to any others being produced. Galileo's instruments could see farther and produce clearer images than others because he was so exacting in the grinding of the lenses for his instruments.

The University of Padua was interested in the instrument and attention it was receiving. Administrators realized that wealthy students would come from all over the world to see the new device and study with its maker, and they wanted to ensure that Galileo would continue to teach at the university. By the end of August 1609 the governors of the university had raised Galileo's salary and offered him a contract for life. As Galileo wrote:

> One of the governors of the University . . . took my hand and told me how that body, knowing the manner in which I had served for seventeen years in Padua . . . [felt] they should renew my appointment for life and with a salary of one thousand florins per year. . . . Thus I find myself here, held for life.[13]

the commercial appeal of this new instrument. Without delay, he took the telescope to Venice to demonstrate its powers to local merchants. People were fascinated by the viewers. In a letter to his brother-in-law on August 29, 1609, Galileo wrote:

> There were a great many gentlemen and senators who, although old, climbed the stairs of the highest bell towers of Venice several times to look for sails on the seas, and ships so far

Galileo took his second telescope to Venice to demonstrate it to local merchants.

Galileo demonstrating his telescope to the Venetian Senate.

The board of governors was correct that the telescope drew attention to the university. Orders were pouring in from rulers and dignitaries around the world. But the governors were incorrect in thinking they would be able to hold Galileo for long.

Gazing Up into the Dark

When the telescope was first built no one thought to use it to observe the night sky. Even Galileo saw it simply as a device to allow one "at sea [to] discover at a much greater distance than usual the hulls and sails of the enemy . . . [to] judge his force, in order to prepare for chase, combat or flight; and likewise, . . . [allow one] on land to look inside fortresses, billets, and defenses of the enemy."[14] But it was only a matter of months before Galileo realized the telescope's greater potential and began using it to study the sky. Historians speculate that a chance glimpse of the rising moon while working with his scope one night at dusk may have inspired Galileo to use the instrument to study the heavens.

According to his notes, Galileo first began making celestial observations in January 1610. What he saw thrilled him. When he turned the scope skyward, hundreds of stars that had been invisible to his

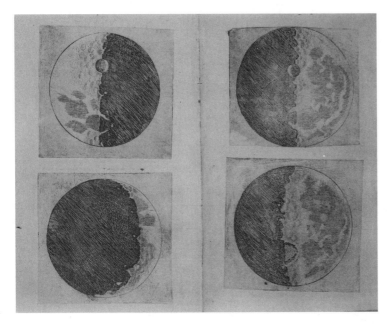

By using his telescope, Galileo was able to make these drawings of the moon.

naked eye seemed to magically appear in the night sky. Galileo wrote in his notes that he was "overwhelmed by the enormous multitude of the stars."

When Galileo turned his telescope toward the moon, he was able to see its mountains and valleys.

With his telescope, Galileo saw things that completely shattered the ideas of Aristotle and Ptolemy, who believed that everything in the heavens was perfectly round and smooth. For example, when he viewed the moon, Galileo discovered that it was covered with mountains and valleys—just like the earth. In his notebook about the moon he wrote:

> Many of the peaks there are in all respects similar to our most rugged and steepest mountains, and among them one can see uninterrupted stretches hundreds of miles long. Others are more in compact groups and there are also many isolated and solitary peaks, precipitous and craggy. But most frequent there are certain ridges . . . very much raised, which surround and enclose plains of different sizes and shape.[15]

By studying the moon, Galileo became convinced that the earth was not a special place set aside for humans by God, as the philosophers and church claimed. Instead it seemed to be similar to other heavenly bodies.

Galileo continued his studies and turned his telescope toward the planet Jupiter. What he saw convinced him that Copernicus was right. By making nightly studies of the planet, he discovered four moons orbiting Jupiter. Galileo reasoned that if Jupiter's four moons could stay in orbit around Jupiter while the planet moved through space, then earth's single moon could orbit it while the earth moved in orbit around the sun. Based on these studies, Galileo concluded that Copernicus's theory was correct. The earth and planets rotated around the sun. Now finally he felt he had proof that the earth was not the fixed center of the universe.

Galileo was quick to share his findings. On January 30, 1610, he wrote to the court of the Duke of Tuscany in Florence:

> I'll infinitely render grace to God that it has pleased him to make me alone the first observer of [a] thing, kept hidden all these ages. That the Moon is a body very similar to the Earth was already ascertained by me.... But, what exceeds all wonders, I have discovered four new planets and observed their ... motions, ... and these new planets move about another very large star [Jupiter] like Venus and Mercury, and [perhaps] the other known planets, move about the Sun.[16]

Following Galileo's example, other scientists began using telescopes to study the heavens. Because so many people were now studying the night sky, Galileo was afraid someone else would duplicate his findings and steal his glory. To prevent this, Galileo rushed to publish his findings.

After looking through his telescope, Galileo decided that Copernicus's theory was correct, and that the earth and other planets revolved around the sun.

The *Starry Messenger*

In March 1610, 550 copies of Galileo's *Sidereus Nuncius (Starry Messenger)* were published. The surviving pages of the original manuscript show that Galileo was indeed hurried. The pages are full of additions and corrections, and in some places slips of paper were inserted after the book was printed to correct errors or make last-minute changes. Nonetheless, the book was an immediate success.

Similarities Between the Planets

Following is a description of Galileo's stellar observations, from a letter to the Tuscan court dated January 1610, and documented in a translation of Galileo's work, the Starry Messenger.

"I am at present in Venice to have printed some observations concerning the heavenly bodies which I have made with one of my spyglasses, and since they are of infinite amazement, I infinitely render grace to God that it has pleased him to make me among the first observers of an admirable thing, kept hidden all these ages. That the Moon is a body very similar to the Earth was already ascertained by me. . . . Besides the Moon, this spyglass has allowed me to discover a multitude of fixed stars never before seen, of which there are more than ten times as many as are naturally visible. Moreover, I have assured myself about what has always been a controversy among the philosophers, that is, what is the Milky Way. But, what exceeds all wonders, I have discovered four new planets and observed their proper and particular motions, different among themselves and from the motions of all the other stars; and these new planets move about another very large star like Venus and Mercury and perchance the other known planets move about the Sun."

In *Starry Messenger* Galileo outlined his findings and made many assertions that supported the Copernican theory, though he was careful not to mention the theory directly. He discussed the great difference in size between stars and planets and drew the conclusion that the stars were much farther away than the planets. Galileo realized that many of his findings shattered long-held beliefs and that his small book would raise a storm of controversy. He did not want to increase the controversy by fully acknowledging his support of Copernicus. Instead he wanted to gently lead people to believe Copernicus's ideas based on the facts he himself discovered through the lens of his telescope.

Starry Messenger was an international success. The British ambassador to the city-state of Venice, Sir Henry Wotton, wrote to his superiors in England on the day the book was printed that a mathematics professor at the University of Padua had discovered new stars shining in the sky, new planets spinning around Jupiter, and mountains hidden on the moon. The professor Galileo, Wotton predicted, was destined to become either exceedingly famous or exceedingly ridiculous. Although news spread much more slowly in the seventeenth century than it does today, copies of the book traveled amazingly fast. It took less than two weeks for copies to travel from Venice to southern Germany and about a month to reach distant England. As soon as Johannes Kepler read *Starry Messenger* he had it reprinted in German. Within two years the book had spread throughout eastern Europe. Within five years of publication, the book was translated into Chinese and was distributed in China. On March 8, 1612, a Polish nobleman, Duke Christopher of Zbaraz, wrote to Galileo:

> Your brilliant [Italian] stars have penetrated all the way to the frigid Muscovite zone. A friend of mine has sent your little book to me from Italy, doing worthy homage to so rare a mind. Ptolemy himself lacked the advantage of possessing all these teachings; our own age, in comparison with that of antiquity, will be celebrated by all. . . . I am very glad that your name will be consecrated to immortality, and honored and admired by everyone.[17]

Many of those who read the book became fascinated with Galileo and his ideas. *Starry Messenger* spurred people to discuss and write about Galileo and his findings. By the close of the century, 405 books had been written about Galileo and his discoveries. People's opinions of Galileo's ideas were almost evenly divided; 160 of these books were favorable to Galileo, 114 were unfavorable, and 131 were neutral.

As people read *Starry Messenger* they began to question the validity of a telescope that showed things not visible to the naked eye. Many Aristotelian scientists claimed that the moons around Jupiter and the mountains Galileo saw on the moon were simply illusions. Galileo's instrument, they declared, deceived the senses.

Galileo's observations of Jupiter and its moons from the Starry Messenger.

Instruments of Torture

An account from Edward Peters's book, Inquisition, *details an early Inquisition trial and the methods used.*

"Of the means or instruments of torture employed in the Tower, there are seven different kinds. The first is the Pit, a subterraneous cave, twenty feet deep and entirely without light. The second is a cell or dungeon so small as to be incapable of admitting a person in erect posture: from its effect on its inmates it has received the name of 'Little Ease.' The third is the rack, on which, by means of wooden rollers and other machinery, the limbs of the sufferer are drawn in opposite directions. The fourth, I believe from the inventor, is called 'The Scavenger's Daughter.' It consists of an iron ring, which brings the head, feet, and hands together, until they form a circle. The fifth is the iron gauntlet, which encloses the hand with the most excruciating pain. The sixth consists of a chain, or manacles, attached to the arms; and the seventh, of fetters, by which the feet are confined."

One of Galileo's loudest critics was Martin Horky, the assistant of his chief rival, astronomer Giovanni Antonio Magini. Horky wrote:

Galileo Galilei, the mathematician of Padua, came to us in Bologna and he brought with him that spyglass through which he sees four fictitious planets. . . . I never slept, day and night, but tested that instrument of Galileo's in innumerable ways, . . . On Earth it works miracles; in the heavens it deceives. . . . All [who looked through the telescope] acknowledged that the instrument deceived.[18]

Even though he failed to convince Magini and Horky, Galileo was sure he could prove that his observations were accurate, if only he could get people to look through his telescope. On March 19, 1610, he wrote to the Tuscan court: "It appears to me necessary . . . to have the truth seen and recognized, by means of the effect itself, by as many people as possible."[19]

Some scientists were willing to accept Galileo's findings without further proof. After reading Horky's statement, Kepler wrote:

I may perhaps seem rash in accepting [Galileo's] claims so readily with no support of my own experience. But why should I not believe a most learned mathematician whose very style attests the soundness of his judgment? He has no intention of practicing deception in

Although Galileo remained in the active city of Venice to study and write about his new astronomical discoveries, he longed to return to his native city of Florence.

a bid for vulgar publicity, nor does he pretend to have seen what he has not seen. Because he loves the truth, he does not hesitate to oppose even the most familiar opinions, and to bear the jeers of the crowd with equanimity.[20]

Horky responded to Kepler's support by publishing an attack against Galileo on June 18, 1610, entitled *A Brief Excursion Against the Starry Messenger*. Horky argued that, since astrologers through the ages had taken into account everything that had any influence on earth or people and had never mentioned moons around Jupiter, the moons could not exist.

One reason some scientists did not believe Galileo is that he carefully guarded the way he built his superior instruments. Few telescopes were powerful enough to show the wonders that Galileo described

in the sky. Even Kepler was unable to prove the existence of moons around Jupiter by use of others' instruments. It was only after he obtained a telescope built by Galileo that he was able to find the moons. After receiving one of Galileo's telescopes he sent a letter: *"Galileae vicisti"* ("You have won, Galileo").[21]

Public Response

While scientists argued about the truth of Galileo's writings, the public embraced his book. The printers in Padua who had printed *Starry Messenger* wrote an ode to Galileo. Other writers published booklets and poems celebrating the telescope and Galileo's discoveries. Italian painter and

Sagredo's Plea

A letter from Galileo's friend, Giovanni Sagredo, and excerpted from Galileo and the Scientific Revolution *written in 1610 begs Galileo to remain in Venice where he will be safe.*

"Where will you find freedom and sovereignty of yourself as in Venice? Especially since you had here support and protection, which became more weighty every day as the age and authority of your friends grew. . . . At present you serve your natural Prince, a great, virtuous man of singular promise; but here you had command over those who command and govern others, and you had to serve only yourself. You were as the ruler of the universe. . . . In a tempestuous sea of a court who can be sure not to be . . . belabored and upset by the furious winds of envy? . . . Who knows what the infinite and incomprehensible events of the world may cause if aided by the impostures of evil and envious men . . . who may even turn the justice and goodness of a prince into the ruin of an honest man? I am very much worried by your being in a place where the authority of the friends of the Jesuits counts heavily."

In 1610, Galileo ignored his friends' advice, and left Venice to return to Florence.

architect Lodovico Cardi da Cigoli painted a fresco honoring Galileo's discoveries in the cupola of the church of Santa Maria Maggiore in Rome. Marino and Chiabrera, leading Italian poets of the day, wrote verses in his honor.

Although the public supported Galileo, the Aristotelians denounced his work. Many refused even to look through a telescope to see if what Galileo said was true or not. In frustration, Galileo wrote to Kepler:

> My dear Kepler what would you say of the learned here who . . . have steadfastly refused to cast a glance through the telescope? What shall we make of all of this? Shall we laugh, or shall we cry?[22]

The fame brought by *Starry Messenger* also brought Galileo an opportunity to return to his native Florence. Two months after publication of his book, Galileo wrote to his friend Belisario Vinta, secretary of state for the city-state of Florence. Galileo spoke of his longing to return to his home and the work he could accomplish if relieved of his teaching duties at Padua.

> I have many and most admirable plans and devices; but they could only be put to work by princes, because it is they who are able to carry on war, build and defend fortresses, and for their regal sport make most splendid expenditure, and not I or any private gentleman. The works that I intend to bring to conclusion are principally two books on the System or Constitution of the World, an immense design full of philosophy, astronomy, and geometry.[23]

Galileo's friends worried about the controversy his book was causing and cautioned him to stay in Venice. Venice could offer him a degree of safety and freedom from the church that he would not have in Florence. His friend Giovanni Sagredo, a Venetian nobleman, wrote:

> Where will you find the same liberty as here in Venetian territory, where a contract makes you the master of those who command? . . . If not ruined, you may be harried by the surging billows of court life and by the raging winds of envy. . . . Also, your being in a place where the authority [of the church], from what I am told, stands high gives me cause for worry.[24]

But the Tuscan court in Florence offered Galileo what he was seeking—the funds and freedom to support his research. In June 1610 Galileo resigned his lifelong post at Padua and was back in Florence by September.

3 A Rising Storm

Galileo arrived in Florence in September 1610 in hope of finding the freedom and peace he needed to continue his experiments and writings. Under his agreement with the Duke of Tuscany, he was expected neither to teach nor even to reside at the University of Pisa, nor at the palace. Galileo was given the titles of Chief Mathematician and Philosopher to the Grand Duke, and Chief Mathematician of the University of Pisa, and he was allowed to live in Florence.

Galileo's salary was more than he had ever made at Padua, and he would no longer have to supplement his income with private tutoring or by manufacturing and selling mathematical instruments.

Galileo continued his observations with his telescope once he arrived in Florence.

Galileo's intent, as he wrote to Vinta, was to focus on the

> many works which I have in mind. These include a great book on the structure of the universe and three books on motion. These last discuss a science I have invented that is so new that its consequences are beyond the wildest imagination. Also, there are books on the principles of machines, on the nature of light and colors, on sound and speech, on the causes of the tides, and on the movements of animals.[25]

More Discoveries in the Night

After his move Galileo continued his observations with the telescope, and the storm of criticism against him continued. The more he discovered, the more he was denounced by scholars and religious leaders. Some scholars argued that the telescope should be banned, because Aristotle would not have approved of the so-called deceptive instrument. Aristotle, they said, had stated that ideas should be derived from unaided sight, and therefore instruments like the telescope were of no use. Galileo

Soon after settling in Florence, Galileo found what he thought were two moons orbiting Saturn. Actually, he had discovered Saturn's rings.

had no patience with his critics and scorned them in public.

> Oh most profound [scholar] . . . [who] will not be led around by Aristotle, but will lead him [Aristotle] by the nose and make him speak as he [the scholar] pleases . . . [they] make themselves willing slaves . . . [and] make an oracle of a wooden image.[26]

Galileo continued his observations of the night skies and made some important discoveries not long after settling in Florence. In observing Saturn he noticed that it appeared to have two moons orbiting it, just as Jupiter had four. He was puzzled by the way these moons seemed to waver in their path around Saturn. Without a more powerful telescope he could not tell that what he had discovered were not moons but the rings of Saturn.

While scanning the night sky Galileo found that Venus seemed to undergo changes similar to the moon's. Sometimes the planet appeared to be shaped like a crescent and at other times it appeared to be a full circle. Watching it closely for weeks, Galileo found that it changed from a whole sphere, to a half, to a quarter, then to a sliver of a sphere, a cycle very similar to that of the moon. He had noted earlier that the phases of the moon were caused by the amount of sunlight striking the moon's surface. He had reasoned that at times the earth blocks the sun's rays and only a small amount of light strikes the moon, making it appear as a crescent. The phases of Venus, Galileo thought, must be caused in a similar way. If this were true it would mean that Venus revolved around the sun and reflected sunlight.

Galileo theorized that when Venus was closest to earth, only a small portion of its

Telescope

In a letter to his brother-in-law written in 1609 as quoted in Stillman Drake's book, Galileo Studies, *Galileo explains how he built his telescope.*

"About ten months ago a report reached my ears that a certain Fleming had constructed a spyglass by means of which visible objects, though very distant from the eye of the observer, were distinctly seen as if nearby. Of this truly remarkable effect several experiences were related, to which some persons gave credence while others denied them. A few days later the report was confirmed to me in a letter from a noble Frenchman at Paris . . . which caused me to apply myself wholeheartedly to inquire into the means by which I might arrive at the invention of a similar instrument. This I did shortly afterwards, my basis being the theory of refraction. First I prepared a tube of lead, at the ends of which I fitted two glass lenses, both planed on one side while on the other side one was spherically concave and the other convex. Then placing my eye near the concave lens, I perceived objects satisfactorily large and near, for they appeared three times closer and nine times larger than when seen with the naked eye alone. Next I constructed another one, more accurate, which represented objects . . . enlarged more than sixty times. I undertook to think about its fabrication; which I finally found, and so perfectly that one which I made far surpassed the reputation of the Flemish one. And word having reached Venice that I had made one, it is six days since I was called by the Signoria, to which I had to show it together with the entire Senate, to the infinite amazement of all; and there have been numerous gentlemen and senators who, though old, have more than once scaled the stairs to the highest [towers] in Venice to observe at sea sails and vessels so far away that, coming under full sail to port, two hours or more were required before they could be seen without my spyglass. For in fact the effect of this instrument is to represent an object that is, for example, fifty miles away, as large and near as if it were only five. Now having known how useful this would be for maritime as well as land affairs, and seeing it desired by the Venetian government, I resolved . . . to appear in the College and make a free gift of it to His Lordship."

Galileo made the drawings of the phases of the moon with the help of his telescope. He later noticed similar patterns in the appearance of Venus.

surface reflected sunlight toward earth. When Venus was farthest away from earth, the sunlight reflected from the entire planet reached earth. This observation contradicted another traditional belief. Before Galileo's discovery people believed that Venus was illuminated with its own light, like a star. If Galileo's theory were correct, Venus revolved around the sun, not the earth. And if this were true, the theory supported by Copernicus was correct and the one supported by Aristotle was false.

Galileo's friends urged him to publish his findings. This would be the perfect proof of Copernicus's writings, they felt. Father Benedetto Castelli, a Catholic scientist and one of Galileo's earliest supporters, wanted him to make his ideas known and silence his critics. Galileo replied, "In order to convince those [stubborn] men who are out for the vain approval of the stupid, . . . it would not be enough even if the stars came down on earth to bring witness about themselves."[27]

Galileo was correct. Even when he released his findings his critics were not convinced. His observations caused an uproar among the followers of Aristotle. What outraged Aristotle's supporters most was that Galileo's findings might be correct. Galileo knew that to challenge any of Aristotle's works would bring the wrath of the universities and the church down on him. In an attempt to make his ideas more acceptable, Galileo pointed out that while Aristotle's logic and reasoning were strong

Galileo's observations of Venus indicated that the planet revolved around the sun, not the earth. This evidence supported Copernicus's theory of a heliocentric solar system.

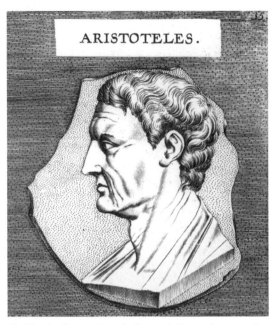

ARISTOTELES.

Galileo's discoveries challenged the ancient teachings of Aristotle.

in some areas, they could be wrong in others. He reasoned that even a great mind like Aristotle's could be in error. Galileo felt Aristotle would have gladly accepted Galileo's arguments if he had known them. Galileo often remarked that Aristotle's followers used his name as a shield to protect them from thinking for themselves. Instead of observing nature and reaching their own conclusions, they relied on Aristotle's authority and denied what they observed in the heavens.

Galileo's Crime

To discredit Galileo his enemies began to spread rumors that he was a heretic who questioned the Bible. The sarcasm with which Galileo answered his critics did not win him support, and the number of people

speaking out against him increased. Soon the university officials at Pisa ordered that none of Galileo's theories or discoveries could be taught or even discussed at the schools. To this Galileo declared that the ignorance of his enemies had always been his best teacher since their blindness forced him to make many experiments to demonstrate the truth of his ideas.

Even though he answered his critics with arrogance and sarcasm, Galileo was alarmed at the whispers that he was a heretic. He tried to explain his beliefs by saying,

> I do not think it necessary to believe that the same God who gave us our sense, our speech, our intellect, would have us put aside the use of these, to teach us instead such things as with their help we could find out for ourselves, particularly in the case of these sciences, of which there is not the smallest mention in the Scriptures.[28]

Galileo knew that being labeled a heretic could cost him his title and position—and maybe even his life. In 1600 scientist Giordano Bruno had been burned to death for supporting scientific ideas contrary to church teachings. As Charles Hummel quotes William Shea, "Individuals and governments were considered subject to a single eternal system of justice based ultimately on eternal and divine law, of which the Catholic church was the sole guardian and interpreter."[29]

Galileo was concerned about the rumors, but he believed that his ideas did not challenge the church or the Bible. Galileo believed that truth could be found both in the Bible and in nature. He wrote, "The Holy Bible and the phenomena of nature proceed alike from the Divine Word. . . . God is known . . . by Nature in

His works, and by His revealed word." Galileo believed the Bible was for saving souls, not to teach science, and that "in discussions of physical problems we [should] begin not from the authority of scriptural passages, but from sense-experience and . . . demonstrations." He felt the purpose of the Bible was to show "how one goes to Heaven, not the way the heavens go."[30]

Giordano Bruno was burned at the stake in 1600 because he supported scientific theories that contradicted church teachings.

Until this time, Galileo had tried to avoid religious controversy. He was a devout Catholic, but he believed that science and religion should be kept separate. In a letter to Father Castelli, he wrote,

> For who would set a limit to the mind of man? Who would dare assert that we know all there is to be known? Therefore, it would be well not to burden the articles concerning salvation and the establishment of the Faith—against which there is no danger that valid contradiction ever may arise—with official interpretations beyond need.[31]

Galileo believed that if the church tried to use the Bible as an authority on scientific theory, it was making a mistake. Galileo believed that eventually all the world would come to accept Copernicus's theories and that the church would be ridiculed for having rejected it. Galileo wrote,

> If [the church] . . . established that to say the earth moves is heresy, and if [later] demonstrations, observations, and . . . experiences show it to move, in what predicament will they have placed the church itself? . . . If the earth moves . . . we cannot change nature and have it not move.[32]

Seeking the Church's Endorsement

Galileo decided he should travel to Rome and explain his theories to the pope, before the voices against him could sway the church's opinion against him. Galileo wanted to obtain an endorsement from the

Galileo used his visit to Rome as an opportunity to demonstrate his astronomical theories.

pope's astronomers in Rome. He felt this endorsement would put an end to his enemies' attempts to discredit him. In April 1611 he arrived in Rome and was received better than he had expected. He wrote to a friend shortly after reaching Rome: "I have been received and [honored] by many illustrious cardinals, prelates, and princes of this city, who wanted to see the things I have observed and were much pleased, as I was too on my part in viewing the marvels of their [city]."[33]

During his stay in Rome Galileo gave many lectures and public demonstrations of his theories. He even presented one of his most powerful telescopes to the pope and spent several nights demonstrating its use. Galileo was very popular with both the rich and the common people in Rome.

Monsignor Piero Dini, one of the Catholic priests at the Vatican during Galileo's stay, wrote to a friend,

He is converting unbelievers one after another. . . . The Lord Cardinal Bellarmine asked the Jesuits for an opinion on Galileo, and the learned Fathers sent the most favorable letter you could think of, and they are great friends of his. . . . The Pope himself had given audience to the astronomer and shown him kindness."[34]

The Academy of the Lynx

Galileo won many supporters, even convincing some staunch supporters of Aristotle to observe the night sky with him. Father Clavius, the foremost Jesuit astronomer, finally agreed that Galileo had discovered new heavenly bodies. Many others in the powerful Jesuit community gave their silent approval and support. But the most important accomplishment of this trip was Galileo's induction into the Lincean Academy.

While lecturing in Rome, Galileo met Prince Frederico Cesi, and the two quickly became friends. Cesi had founded a society dedicated to promoting science. The group was called the Lincean Academy (Academy of the Lynx) named after the lynx because of the animal's excellent eyesight. The group's charter stated that the academy "desired as its members philosophers who are eager for real knowledge." The members came from a variety of backgrounds and their scientific interests were in many different areas. The group was frustrated by the lack of scientific investigation at universities and the resistance of most scholars to explore new ideas. The common goal of the group was "to fight Aristotelism all the way," according to Cesi.

The academy was important because it was the first scientific society in the world and served as a model for most modern groups. The society also gave scientists a

The title page of Galileo's most famous writing, Dialogue on the Great World Systems.

way to share their ideas and a forum to test their experiments. After joining the academy, Galileo began a long correspondence with Cesi. Through this friendship, and membership in the society, Galileo's ideas were transmitted throughout Europe. Also, due to his position in Rome, Cesi was able to keep his friend informed of the church's opinion of him. The academy was able to use what power it had to shield Galileo from his critics and to publish some of his later works. Without their help, his most famous work, *Dialogue on the Great World Systems,* might never have been published. And the academy benefited because Galileo's reputation brought prestige and attracted other famous scientists to the new group.

The Lincean Academy

The creed of the Lincean Academy, printed in 1603 and excerpted from Stillman Drake's book, Galileo Studies, *explains the purpose behind the world's first science academy. The Linceans wanted to create an organization dedicated to mathematics and science and free from all political controversy.*

"The Lincean Academy desires as its members philosophers who are eager for real knowledge, and who will give themselves to the study of nature, and especially to mathematics; at the same time, it will not neglect the ornaments of elegant literature and philology, which like graceful garments, adorn the whole body of science. . . . It is not within the Lincean plan to find leisure for recitations and debate; meetings will be neither frequent nor lengthy, and chiefly for the transaction of necessary business of the academy; but those who wish to enjoy such exercises will not be hindered in any way, so long as they perform them as incidental studies, decently and quietly, and not as vain promises and professions of how much they are about to accomplish. For there is ample philosophical employment for everyone by himself, particularly if pains are taken in the observation of natural phenomena and the book of nature which is always at hand; this is, the heavens and the earth. . . . Let members add to their names the title of Lincean, which has been chosen as a caution and a constant stimulus, especially when they write on any literary subject, or in their private letters to associates, and in general when any work is wisely and well performed. . . . The Linceans will pass over in silence all political controversies and every kind of quarrels and wordy disputes, especially gratuitous ones which give occasion to deceit, unfriendliness and hatred, as men who desire peace and seek to preserve their studies from molestation and would avoid any sort of disturbance. And if anyone by command of his superiors or some other requirement shall be reduced to handling of such questions, let those be printed without the name of Lincean, since they are alien to physical and mathematical science and hence to the objects of the Academy."

The emblem of the Lincean Academy.

Spots on the Sun

Galileo left Rome, basking in his success, but he was soon to need all of his friends' support. Shortly after returning to Florence, Galileo made an enemy of Christopher Scheiner, a prominent Jesuit astronomer. The Jesuits were the scientific arm of the Catholic church, and they were extremely powerful during Galileo's time. In 1612 Scheiner wrote several letters to another distinguished astronomer, Mark Welser, announcing his discovery of sunspots. Scheiner believed the sunspots were small planets that circled around the sun.

When Welser published Scheiner's letters, Galileo immediately replied with several letters. He stated that he had discovered sunspots earlier but had not published anything on them, as he wanted to observe them further. Galileo went on to ridicule Scheiner's theories and to propose that the

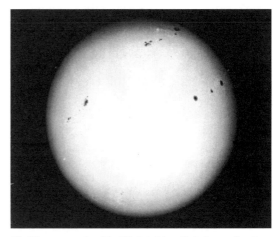

Galileo argued with Christopher Scheiner about the origin of sunspots.

spots were clouds that were on the surface of the sun itself. (It was an important distinction to Galileo that the spots he had observed were on the surface of the sun, for this was another example of the imperfection and changeability of heavenly bodies.) Galileo was so furious with what he

An illustration of the study of sunspots from Christopher Scheiner's writings.

An Appeal to All

In this excerpt from Stillman Drake's Galileo Studies, *Galileo writes to his friend Paolo Gualdo in 1612 explaining that science should be available to everyone, not just those fortunate or rich enough to attend a university.*

"I notice that young men go to the universities in order to become doctors or philosophers or anything so long as it is a title and that many go in for those professions who are utterly unfit to them, while others who would be very competent are prevented by business or their daily cares which keep them away from letters. Now these people, while provided with a good intelligence, yet, because they cannot understand what is written in [Latin] retain through life the idea that those big folios contain matters beyond their capacity which will forever remain closed to them; whereas I want them to realize that nature, as she has given them eyes to see her works, has given them a brain apt to grasp and understand them."

perceived as Scheiner's theft of his discovery that he wrote a scathing refutation of Scheiner's theories. This made Scheiner look foolish, and his fellow Jesuits rushed to his defense. Galileo answered with more biting wit and hard-to-refute arguments, insulting the entire Jesuit community in the process.

Galileo had been on the unpopular side of an argument before, and enjoyed a lively debate, but now his challenges went too far. Many of the Jesuits had sided with Scheiner, and those who had not were reluctant to speak up in support of Galileo. This time Galileo had written something that brought him in direct conflict with a powerful and respected member of the church. Galileo's works could no longer be ignored, and his enemies began to plot his downfall.

Chapter

4 Facing the Church's Wrath

Galileo's discoveries and his support of Copernicus's theories soon brought him to the attention of church leaders. On December 20, 1614, Tommaso Caccini preached a fiery sermon against Galileo and Copernicus. Caccini was a Dominican, the most conservative branch of the Catholic church. The Dominicans referred to themselves as the "watchdogs of the faith," and they were particularly watchful of philosophers who meddled in theology.

Galileo (below) and his discoveries were condemned by Tommaso Caccini, a Dominican priest.

Caccini used his sermon to stir up the church leaders. He shocked the people of Florence by calling the Copernican theories and mathematics the work of the devil and by publicly suggesting that Galileo's ideas about a moving earth and a stationary sun were heresy. He rebuked Galileo's supporters, saying "Ye men of Galilee, why stand ye gazing up into heaven?"

These were strong words from Caccini, as Giorgio de Santillana points out in his book *The Crime of Galileo:*

> Although it was not infrequent to have preachers in their zeal upbraid academic learning and the pride of universities, it was not done to start shouting heresy and damnation from the pulpit until and unless the correct position had been defined by Rome; and it was well known that the authorities were keeping an open mind about the new discoveries.[35]

Caccini hoped to "create a scandal and uproar centered around the person of Galileo and thus compel the Roman authorities, always very sensitive on the subject of 'scandal,' to take for reasons of public order the measures that they seemed reluctant to take on the grounds of theory."[36] Caccini planned to show the arrogant Galileo the power of the church—and especially that of the Dominicans.

Soon after Caccini's sermon Galileo received a letter of warning from his friend Monsignor Giovanni Ciampoili. The monsignor informed Galileo that he had heard of Caccini's sermon and "though not everything is to be feared, . . . nothing is to be disregarded. . . . It is indeed true that one must always remember that men are bitter, like people in hard battle, in these matters in which the friars usually do not wish to lose." He also cautioned Galileo that his "little phrase about submitting yourself ever to the . . . Church can never be too often repeated."[37]

Galileo was amazed and a bit alarmed by the sermon and Ciampoili's letter. Other friends and patrons in Rome reassured him, however, that the sermon reflected the views of a small group of Dominicans who were trying to get attention from Rome and were not the views of the church itself. The head of the Dominicans, Father Maraffi, wrote a formal letter to Galileo in which he apologized for "all the idiocies that [the monks under his leadership] may and do actually commit."[38] Tommaso Caccini's own brother Matteo, who was a Dominican in the Vatican, was furious when he heard about the sermon. Matteo wrote to his brother:

I hear of such greatly extravagant antics on your part that I am amazed and disgusted beyond measure. It may yet come to . . . pass that you'll regret ever having learned to read. You could have done nothing more annoying to the high authorities here, up to the very highest. . . . It is no use your draping yourself with the mantle of zeal and religion, because here [in Rome] everybody knows how you [monks] use such cover. . . . Truly it is a great impertinence. . . . I ask that you stop preaching. . . . You have behaved like a dreadful fool.[39]

A Conspiracy

Galileo was reassured. But he should not have been. In fact, a group of conservative Dominicans and Jesuits contacted the archbishop of Pisa and urged him to begin investigating Galileo as an enemy of the church. Some of the university professors Galileo had offended and embarrassed over the years joined in making the request.

In March 1613 Galileo received a letter from his friend Father Benedetto Castelli. Castelli wrote to report an incident that had greatly disturbed him. At a court dinner Castelli had been challenged by Grand Duchess Christina of Lorraine. She was very concerned about the teaching of Copernican astronomy. She had been told by some of the professors in Florence that such teaching was against what was written in the Bible. Castelli had tried to defend Copernicus's ideas to her but urged Galileo to speak to her himself. He believed that this had been a deliberate attempt by Galileo's enemies to arouse the religious authorities against him and that it demanded Galileo's immediate attention.

Galileo was troubled by Castelli's letter. He had tried to avoid any comparison between his discoveries and biblical writings. He was adamant in his belief that religious truths and scientific truths were separate and did not contradict one another. Galileo felt that he could prove, through reason and logic, that the ideas of Copernicus did not contradict the church's teachings.

In His Own Defense

Because Grand Duchess Christina was the mother of Galileo's patron, Grand Duke Cosimo of Tuscany, Galileo wanted to explain his ideas to her. Galileo composed his famous "Letter to Madam Christina of Lorraine." In it he attempted to explain three important issues: First, that Copernicus's theories did not disagree with the Bible unless the Bible was taken literally—something that was not traditionally done. Second, that his opponents were bringing their case to church authorities because of their envy and bitterness toward Galileo, not because they believed his support of Copernicus's ideas to be against the church: They "have resolved to fabricate a shield for their fallacies of the mantle [cloak] of pretended religion and the authority of the Bible. These they apply, with little judgment, to the refutation of arguments that they do not understand and have not even listened to." Third, he maintained that questions of science could not and should not be considered questions of faith. He was not pleased with men who were "of profound learning and devout behavior, but who nevertheless [try to force] others by scriptural authority to follow . . . that opinion which they think best agrees with the Bible, and then believe themselves not bound to answer the opposing reasons and experiences."[40]

Although Galileo worded his letter carefully and respectfully, the statements he made were radical ones. He knew that some of the things he had written could be controversial, but he also had great faith in his powers of persuasion. He sent a copy of the letter to Father Castelli in Pisa, who quickly showed it around the university.

Nicolaus Copernicus argued the existence of a heliocentric universe. Galileo explained and defended this theory in the "Letter to Madam Christina of Lorraine."

Castelli thought Galileo's arguments were so clear and logical that the university professors would have to agree with him. Unfortunately, the envious professors used parts of Galileo's letter as proof that he was criticizing the church. The clergy were quick to condemn Galileo as a heretic by claiming he was attempting to interpret the Bible, something that only the church was allowed to do. This was a serious attack and one that even Galileo could not ignore.

Galileo decided that his best course of action would be to make a second trip to Rome. There he could explain to church authorities his own theories and the scientific truths of Copernicus in person. He believed that his reputation and his persuasive speaking was necessary to convince

A Condemning Letter

After reading Galileo's letter to Father Benedetto Castelli in 1615, in which Galileo outlines some of his ideas, Father Nicolo Lorini writes to the Inquisition warning them of Galileo's ideas. The letter is excerpted from Giorgio de Santillana's book, The Crime of Galileo.

"All our Fathers of this devout convent of St. Mark are of the opinion that the letter contains many propositions which appear to be suspicious or presumptuous, as when it asserts that the language of the Holy Scripture does not mean what it seems to mean; that in discussions about natural phenomena the last and lowest place ought to be given to the authority of the sacred text [Bible]; that its commentators have very often erred in their interpretation; that the Holy Scriptures should not be mixed up with anything except matters of religion . . . that in Nature philosophical and astronomical evidence is of more value than holy and divine (Which passages your Lordship will find underlined by me in the said letter, of which I send an exact copy); and finally that, when Joshua commanded the Sun to stand still, we must understand that the command was addressed [only to the earth] . . . when I saw that they . . . strove to defend an opinion which appeared to be quite contrary to the [Bible]; . . . that they were treading underfoot the entire philosophy of Aristotle. . . . I made up my mind to acquaint your Lordship with the state of affairs, that you in your holy zeal . . . may . . . provide remedies as will appear advisable."

church authorities to consider Copernicus's ideas. He had long ago given up the idea of convincing the Aristotelians but still had hope for the church. As he wrote to his friend Monsignor Dini:

> How can all my labors fail to be in vain if those [followers of Aristotle] who must be persuaded show themselves incapable of understanding even the simplest and easiest arguments? . . . Yet I should not despair of overcoming even this difficulty if I were in a position to use my tongue in place of my pen . . . so that I can go there . . . showing my affection for the Holy Church.[41]

His friends tried to persuade him not to go to Rome. Many felt that his presence would pressure the church into taking a firm stand against Copernicanism in any form. Others felt that Galileo himself was in danger—or soon would be if he continued to draw the attention of the Dominicans.

Cardinal Roberto Bellarmine, from whom the pope received most of his scientific advice, was very friendly toward the Dominicans. The Dominicans in turn had the ear of Inquisition authorities and were already encouraging them to call an informal hearing on Galileo's theories.

The Inquisition was an organization of monks whose power was absolute. It often played the role of accuser, judge, jury and executioner for those suspected of heresy. During the Renaissance the Inquisition's methods became harsher as they fought to stop the flood of ideas that was threatening the foundations of the church's authority. Judges often used torture and punishments, including life imprisonment and burning at the stake, to force confessions.

Piero Guicciardini, the Florentine ambassador to Rome, advised Galileo not to press his case in Rome. He sent a letter stating his misgivings to Curzio Picchena, a member of the grand duke's court, saying:

> I hear that Galileo is coming. . . . When
> I first came here [in 1611] he was

Cardinal Roberto Bellarmine advised the pope on scientific matters.

During the Inquisition, many people were burned at the stake for suspected heresy.

Galileo was convinced that if he demonstrated the truth of his writings, that the church would not condemn him.

here, and spent some days in the house. His views, and something else too, did not please the advisers and cardinals of the Holy Office. Among others, Bellarmine told me that . . . if he was here too long, nothing less could be done than to arrive at some judgment concerning his affairs.

I do not know if he has changed his views or his temper, but I know very well that some Dominicans who play a great part in the Holy Office, as well as others, are ill-disposed toward him, and this is no place to come to argue about the moon, nor [at this time], to support . . . any new doctrines.[42]

Galileo, however, remained optimistic. He was certain that when shown the truth, the church couldn't help but support him. As Professor Ludovico Geymonat writes in his book *Galileo Galilei,* Galileo launched a "plan to obtain for the new science the favor and support of all the powerful men of the world, from princes to the Church itself." Galileo considered science not as a private activity of individual scholars but "as a matter of public interest that was destined to [influence] all society." Galileo was very aware of the power and influence of the church, and he was convinced that "he must try by every means to convert the church to the cause of science, in order to prevent any rupture between the two that might dangerously retard the development of scientific research."[43]

A Trip to Rome

Galileo traveled to Rome in December 1615. During his three-month visit he was treated with the utmost respect and honor by church officials. The grand duke of Florence actively supported his mission and sent letters ahead to smooth the way. Galileo spent his time lecturing on his theories and giving public demonstrations of his telescope. He was a great showman and a fiery public speaker and drew great crowds wherever he lectured. Antonio Querengo, who was in Rome during Galileo's stay, wrote to Cardinal Allesandro d'Este:

Your Eminence would take great pleasure in Galileo if you could hear him [debate], as he does often among fifteen or twenty who attack him cruelly. . . . But he is fortified in such a way as to laugh at them all, and although he does not convince people of his new opinion, he nevertheless vanquishes most of the arguments by which his opponents seek to crush him. . . . He gave marvelous proofs, and . . . before replying to the opposing arguments he amplified and strengthened them with new supports of apparently great magnitude, in order, when he demolished them, to make the adversaries look even more ridiculous.[44]

The public was delighted to see some of the stuffy, arrogant scholars embarrassed and at a loss for words. But while Galileo entertained the crowds many of the eminent scholars that he ridiculed were

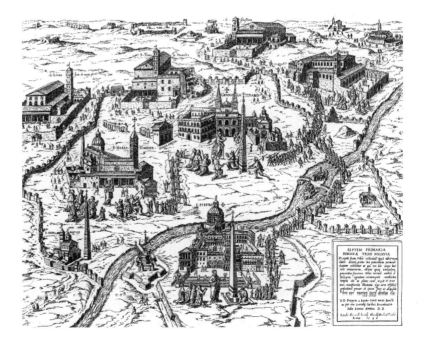

Galileo went to Rome in 1615 to lecture and demonstrate his theories.

A Tense Reception

In a letter home written on January 8, 1616, and excerpted from Giorgio de Santillana's book, The Crime of Galileo, *Galileo describes his reception in Rome.*

"My business is far more difficult, and takes much longer owing to outward circumstances, than the nature of it would require; because I cannot communicate directly with those persons with whom I have to negotiate, partly to avoid doing injury to my friends, partly because they cannot communicate anything to me without running the risk of grave censure. And so I am compelled, with much pains and caution, to seek out third persons, who, without even knowing my object, may serve as mediators with the principals, so that I may have the opportunity of setting forth . . . the particulars of my interest. I have also to set down some points in writing, and to cause that they should come privately into the hands of those whom I wish should see them; for I find in many quarters that people are more ready to yield to dead writing than to living speech, for the former permits them to agree or dissent without blushing, and then finally to yield to the arguments used—since in such discussions we have no witnesses but ourselves, whereas people do not so readily change their opinions when it has to be done publicly."

sending details of his activities to the Inquisition. Church officials were alarmed. They were concerned that Galileo's radical ideas might lead other people to question the church's authority to define the roles of rulers, scientists, and religious leaders. They felt that the church had to take a firm stand or watch more of its power slip away.

For nearly two months the officials of the Inquisition questioned scholars and clergy about Galileo and his ideas. A panel of clergymen called the Congregation of the Index decided which books should be forbidden or corrected. They summarized Galileo's theories in an understandable form:

"That the sun is the center of the universe, and consequently is not moved by any local motion; That the earth is not the center of the universe nor is it motionless, but moves as a whole, and also with [a daily] motion."[45]

After this report the panel quickly reached a decision about Galileo. They stated that the belief that the sun does not move was foolish and contradicted the Bible. They also judged that the belief that the earth moved was "stupid and absurd" as it could easily be seen by anyone standing on the earth that it was not moving.

Forbidden Words

When Galileo was called before Cardinal Bellarmine on February 25, 1616, he thought he would be allowed to explain his theories. He had eagerly awaited this meeting and felt well prepared to state the case for Copernicanism. Galileo still naively believed that the problem was ignorance, not politics. He was wrong.

The meeting with Bellarmine was short and to the point. Galileo was informed that the pope had ordered him not to hold, teach, or defend the Copernican system. The works of Copernicus were to be prohibited. The entire Copernican theory was judged "contrary to Holy Scripture and therefore cannot be defended."

Galileo could hardly believe what had happened. He stayed in Rome for three months after his meeting with Bellarmine to assess how rigidly the restrictions would be enforced. Galileo felt sure that, given time, the church would relax some of its restrictions. Through his powerful friends Galileo arranged an audience with the pope to try once more to explain his theories. The pope treated him kindly but was unmovable. The church's judgment on Copernicus, and thus on Galileo, was final. This was a terrible setback for Galileo. He had planned to write a great book comparing the Ptolemaic and Copernican systems. Now he was forbidden to even speak on the subject. His own powerful position had been shaken, and people avoided him. Rumors quickly began that Galileo had renounced his beliefs to Cardinal Bellarmine. Some said that he had been punished and that his own writings would soon be prohibited. None of this was true, but it tarnished Galileo's reputation and hurt his pride. He sought out yet another audience with Cardinal Bellarmine and asked him to make a written statement denouncing these lies. Bellarmine agreed and wrote:

> We, Robert Cardinal Bellarmine, having heard that Signor Galileo Galilei is [said] to have [renounced his beliefs before us], and even of having been given . . . penance for this; and . . . we say that the said Signor Galilei has not renounced any opinion or doctrine of his [before us or to] anyone else at Rome, much less anywhere else, . . . nor has he received penance of any sort; but has only been told the decision made by His Holiness in which it is declared that the doctrine attributed to Copernicus, that the earth moves round the sun and that the sun is fixed in the center of the universe without is contrary to the Holy Scriptures, and therefore cannot be defended or held. And in witness of this we have written and signed this with our own hand.[46]

These strong words from Cardinal Bellarmine carried all the weight of the church. Galileo felt that his reputation was salvaged and he could return to Florence without shame. He began to consider the church's decision as only a temporary setback. Although discouraged, he was not ready to give up trying to convince the church of the truth of his theories.

Public Dismay

Others were more disheartened by the church's actions. Fellow scientists who supported Copernicus's theories believed that

Johannes Kepler (left) supported Copernicus's ideas privately. The scientist thought that Galileo had caused great harm to science by forcing the church to make a decision about Copernicus's theory.

Galileo had caused great damage by forcing the church to rule on Copernicus. Even Kepler, a long-time admirer of Galileo, wrote: "Some, through their impudent behavior, have brought things to such a point that the reading of the work of Copernicus, which remained absolutely free for eighty years, is now prohibited until that work is corrected." Some feared for Galileo's personal safety. The Florentine ambassador wrote to the grand duke, "I know that there are here at the Holy Office and elsewhere certain Dominicans who are ill-disposed toward Galileo. . . . One of these days we shall hear that he has fallen over a steep [cliff]."[47]

Upon his return to Florence, Galileo's friends and supporters were able to convince him to let the controversy and rumors die down and to concentrate on other studies. Galileo was despondent for a short time, writing to his friends that he had lost his battle to "those three most powerful operators, ignorance, malice and impiety." But, even though the church had rejected his work, Galileo could not turn his back on science. He soon was hard at work drafting new longitude calculation tables for sailors based on his studies of Jupiter. He worked on complicated mathematical problems and on his theories of why the tides rose and fell. While he did not write or speak of Copernicus's theories, he did take every opportunity to criticize Aristotle and his supporters.

The Assayer

Galileo wrote some of his most scathing attacks on Aristotle and his supporters in 1618 when three new comets appeared. The comets were an exciting event, and many scholars quickly published treatises speculating on their origin. Galileo feared he might offend church authorities further if he published or publicly discussed his own ideas about the comets. But he could not sit quietly while other scholars were making ridiculous statements about the comets. So Galileo secretly helped his student Mario Guiducci write and publish a lengthy essay called *A Discourse on Comets,* which presented Galileo's own opinions. Guiducci's writings were well received, and even Cardinal Maffeo Barberini, a rich nobleman and a powerful member of the church, commented favorably on them. Cardinal Barberini prided himself on his scientific knowledge and support of scientific studies. Barberini had met Galileo during one of the scientist's visits to Rome, and the two had become friends. Having Barberini's support was a major victory for Galileo. Galileo was encouraged by this response and began work on a new booklet called *The Assayer.*

The Assayer is one of Galileo's most important works. It is a sharp and stinging

When three new comets appeared in 1618, Galileo took the opportunity to publish his ideas about comets.

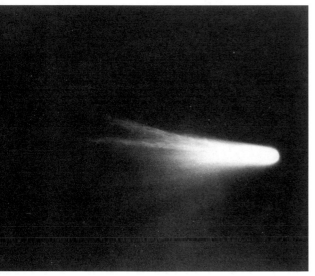

critique of the ideas being promoted by the Jesuits and the university professors about the nature of comets. But more importantly, according to Ludovico Geymonat in *Galileo Galilei,* it clearly explains Galileo's views on scientific method and his deep belief that knowledge gained by direct experience was superior to knowledge based only on the authority of others. This was a new way of thinking about people and their experiences, and it captured the attention of other scientists and amateur astronomers. In *The Assayer,* Galileo scolded his enemies, saying that no proof, no matter how solid, would convince them. Instead, Galileo claimed, his opponents were determined to believe the authority of dead poets and philosophers instead of the scientific evidence he produced. In the book, he further explained his attitude toward his job as a scientist as one of asking the kinds of questions that make people look for new answers. Galileo felt that even questions already answered should be reexamined occasionally, and that by doing so all the possible answers to a question would eventually be found. This is what Galileo called the discovery of truth.

With the publication of *The Assayer,* Galileo was once again in the public eye. He could not have chosen a better time to break his silence and begin writing again. At the time *The Assayer* was being printed by the Lincean Academy, word reached Galileo that a new pope was elected. Galileo was overjoyed to find that it was his friend Cardinal Barberini. He and leaders of the Lincean Academy immediately wrote a lengthy letter dedicating *The Assayer* to the new pope. This quieted the most vocal of Galileo's opponents, who had been attempting to keep *The Assayer* from being published.

Reaction to *The Assayer*

In 1619 Galileo's friend Mario Guiducci wrote from Rome to inform Galileo how The Assayer *was received by the church. This excerpt is from Giorgio de Santillana's book,* The Crime of Galileo.

"First, some months ago at the Congregation of the Holy Office, a pious person proposed to prohibit or correct *The Assayer,* charging that it praised the doctrine of Copernicus with respect to the earth's motion: as to which matter a cardinal assumed the task of informing himself about the situation and reporting it; and by good fortune he happened to hand over the case to Father Guevara, father general of some sort. . . . He read the work diligently and, having enjoyed it very much, praised and celebrated it greatly to that cardinal, and besides put on paper certain defenses, according to which that doctrine of motion, even it were held, did not seem to him to be condemnable; and so the matter quieted down for the moment. Now, not having this support from that cardinal who could help us, it does not seem that we should run the risk of a scolding; for . . . Copernicus's opinion is defended . . . and although it states openly that with the assistance of a superior light it is proven false, all the same the malicious will not see it thus and will get into an uproar again; and as we lack the protection of His Excellency Cardinal Barberino, who is absent, and further having as an opponent in this matter another important gentleman, who was once one of the first to defend it, and furthermore [the authorities] being very annoyed by these . . . intrigues so that one cannot talk to him about it, it would definitely remain up to the discretion and intelligence of the friars. For all these reasons, it seemed to me right, as I said, to let the matter sleep for a while, rather than keeping it alive with persecutions and having to ward off those who can deliver some sly blows. Meanwhile, time will help our case."

Barberini, or Pope Urban VIII as he was renamed, was flattered by the dedication. He referred often to Galileo's wonderful writing and took pride in extending to Galileo and the Lincean Academy his "most benign protection." Galileo had high hopes that the new pope would set the church on the road to scientific enlightenment.

Back to Rome

Prince Federico Cesi sent several letters of encouragement and assurances that Urban was eager to talk with Galileo. Galileo arrived again in Rome early in 1624. He was received with great warmth and affection by Urban, who would not even allow Galileo to kneel before him. Urban showered him with small gifts, dinners, and other honors. He promised Galileo a pension and showed him genuine affection and respect during all of their meetings. Galileo was treated so well that he stayed in Rome for over six weeks, enjoying a private audience with the pope each week.

While Galileo's time with the pope was filled with pleasant conversation, he was unable to convince Urban to relax the church's restrictions on Copernicus's work. Galileo soon found that although his friend Maffeo Barberini loved to debate and speculate on Copernicus's theories, as the pope he would not use his power to change the church's ruling. After many weeks Urban granted Galileo permission to write a book comparing the different theories of the universe. But he cautioned Galileo that the Copernican system must not be presented as a fact, only as a theory. Galileo must not write anything that might contradict the Scriptures. Urban pointed out that the church would not reverse its decision on Copernicanism, and Galileo should be careful not to appear to be challenging that decision.

Although Galileo had not been able to have the decisions of 1616 reversed, he had been granted permission to write his

Pope Urban VIII initially encouraged Galileo's work.

long-planned book. He interpreted Urban's decision to allow him to write his book to mean that the church would look the other way as long as Galileo was discreet and did not openly challenge Rome's authority. He took this as a sign that the church was at last willing to listen. To Galileo, this was his great opportunity to bring enlightenment to the church and the scientific community.

He left for Florence in June 1624 to begin writing his greatest work. Galileo had been planning this book for over two decades. Now, finally, after all his setbacks, he would bring to the world Copernicus's grand vision of the universe.

5 Dialogue

Galileo returned to Florence with mixed emotions. Although laden with holy medals and a papal letter of commendation to the grand duke in which Urban wrote, "We embrace with paternal love this great man whose fame shines in the heavens and goes on earth far and wide," Galileo was disappointed that he had not obtained permission to write about the Copernican theory as the truth. Galileo had dreamed that Italy and the Catholic church would blaze new scientific trails and remain the intellectual leaders of the world. But Urban's refusal to sanction the Copernican theory dashed his hopes that the church would become a leading force in science. Galileo was still hopeful that even if he could not rouse the church to support Copernicanism, he could stop it from supporting the adversaries of science.

Even though Galileo claimed that Urban supported his new book, Galileo's friends were worried. Urban was known as a passionate and unpredictable man. He was ambitious for power and jealous of anyone who tried to take away his authority. Galileo's friends urged him to wait until Urban granted official permission for the book, preferably in writing. Galileo responded that his life was too short to sit around forever and wait for busy officials to change their minds. He was growing old and his health was failing. If he were to write his book he must do it now.

A Dialogue

Galileo began writing in 1624. He decided to write the book in the form of a dialogue among three friends. This form would allow him to introduce a wide variety of subjects and ideas without being personally responsible for them. He wrote to a friend who had embraced Protestantism and moved to Paris. "I have taken up work again on the [book]. . . . With God's grace I have found the right line, which ought to allow me to terminate it within the winter; it will provide I trust, a most ample confirmation of the Copernican system."[48] After years of work the book was finished in January 1630.

During Galileo's lifetime all books had to be approved by the Catholic church before they were published. Galileo sent his manuscript to Rome to Father Nicolo Riccardi, the chief licenser, and his assistant Father Rafael Visconti, who were given the task of editing Galileo's book and ensuring it did not contain heresy. Father Riccardi read the text and was uneasy. Riccardi did not know a lot about astronomy, but the book seemed to support the forbidden subject of Copernicanism. Before Riccardi would give his permission he had the book reviewed by church mathematicians and by members of the Inquisition. Each body approved it with only minor changes. But Riccardi still was uneasy and delayed approving the book. During this time Galileo wrote to a friend, "the months and years pass, my life wastes away, and my work is condemned to rot." Finally, Riccardi could delay no more, and on July 19, 1631, he sent his last changes to the Inquisitor at Florence: Father Giacinto Stefani, who was

The frontispiece for Galileo's Dialogue of Galileo Galilei wherein the meetings of four days, are discussed the two chief systems of the world, Ptolemaic and Copernican.

in charge of the Inquisition in the city of Florence. Stefani read the book and found nothing wrong with it. Stefani wrote that he was "moved to tears at many of the passages by the humility and reverent obedience displayed by the author."[49]

Galileo was encouraged by Stefani's remarks, and he willingly accepted all of Riccardi's changes without question. Finally, after more delays while Galileo waited for the preface, which was being written under the pope's direction, the book emerged on February 21, 1632, from the Florentine press of Landini. The book was officially called *Dialogue of Galileo Galilei wherein the meetings of four days, are discussed the two chief systems of the world, Ptolemaic and Copernican.*

The book contained the lively arguments of three friends: Salviati, named for Galileo's friend, the Florentine nobleman Filippo Salviati; Sagredo, named for the Venetian nobleman Giovanni Sagredo; and Simplicio, named for an ancient philosopher. In the dialogue Simplicio supports Aristotle's beliefs, Salviati supports Copernicus, and Sagredo plays the role of the intellectual nobleman they are both trying to win to their point of view. The book is divided into four sections that cover a period of four days. On the first day the three men discuss Aristotle, specifically his idea that the earth is the center of the universe. The second and third days are devoted to Copernicus's ideas and the religious arguments against the notion that the earth moves. The fourth day is devoted to discussing the ebb and flow of the seas, which Galileo felt were caused by the earth's rotation and travel around the sun.

Throughout the book Salviati makes strong arguments for Copernicus's ideas. Often Simplicio is forced to retreat to religious arguments. For example, when the

Nature Is as God Willed It

"Let Us grant you that all of your demonstrations are sound and that it is entirely possible for things to stand as you say. But now tell Us, do you really maintain that God could not have wished or known how to move the heavens and the stars in some other way: We suppose you will say 'Yes,' because We do not see how you could answer otherwise. Very well then, if you still want to save your contention, you would have to prove to Us that, if the heavenly movements took place in another manner than the one you suggest, it would imply a logical contradiction at some point, since God in His infinite power can do anything that does not imply a contradiction. Are you prepared to prove as much? No? Then you will have to concede to Us that God can, conceivably, have arranged things in an entirely different manner, while yet bringing about the effects that We see. And if this possibility exists, which might still preserve in their literal truth the sayings of Scripture, it is not for us mortals to try to force those holy words to mean what to Us, from here, may appear to be the solution. . . . To speak otherwise than hypothetically on the subject would be tantamount to constraining the infinite power and wisdom of God within the limits of your personal ideas."

Pope Urban VIII disapproved of the conclusions Galileo drew from his observations.

three men discuss the ocean tides, Simplicio has no counterargument to Salviati's. Instead he replies

> As to the discourse we have held, and especially this last one concerning the reasons for the ebbing and flowing of the ocean, I am really not entirely convinced. . . . I know that if asked whether God in his infinite power and wisdom could have conferred upon the [ocean] its observed motion using some other means . . . both of you would reply that He could have, and that He would have known how to do this in many ways which are unthinkable to our minds. From this I forthwith conclude it would be excessive boldness for anyone to limit and restrict the Divine power and wisdom to some particular fancy of his own.[50]

Simplicio echoes an argument that is very similar to a speech Urban once made to Galileo when telling him his investigation into nature was foolish. Galileo was careful to alter this argument so that it would not appear to be a direct comment on the pope's beliefs. Simplicio argues that the universe is exactly how God has made it and that people cannot make up rules to explain anything created by God. Simplicio states that the universe works as it does simply because God wills it to be so. In *Dialogue,* Galileo answers such arguments by saying,

> Surely, God could have caused birds to fly with their bones made of solid gold, with their veins full of quicksilver, with their flesh heavier than lead, and with wings exceeding small. He did not, and that ought to show something. It is only in order to shield your ignorance that you put the Lord at every turn to the refuge of a miracle.[51]

Public Reaction

The book was greeted with great praise. Many scientists and lay people loved it, and the first edition sold out as it came off the press. One scientist wrote of it, "These novelties of ancient truths, of new world, new systems, new nations, are the beginning of a new era."[52]

Dialogue also was a triumph because it explained Copernicus's ideas in a way that everyone could understand. Copernicus's original work was long, unwieldy, and written in Latin for scientists. Kepler's books were even more confusing and were also written in Latin. Galileo, on the other hand, wrote in Italian so that all of his countrymen could read what he wrote. His witty and easy-to-understand writing made the book very popular. As scientist Fulgenzao Micanzio said after reading it, "And who before now had guessed what the Copernican issue was all about?"[53]

Storm Clouds Gather

Galileo's appeal to the public alarmed some authorities, however. Normally a scientific work would not have generated much controversy outside of universities because it would be read only by other scholars. Academic disputes among mathematicians or astronomers were tolerated by politicians and the church because these arguments had little effect on the world outside of the colleges. By writing in

A Better Reasoner

The Assayer, *printed in 1618, was one of Galileo's fiercest attacks on Aristotle. In the following passage, excerpted from Giorgio de Santillana's book,* The Crime of Galileo, *he ridicules people's desire to follow ancient authorities.*

"I cannot refrain from marveling that [other scientists] will persist in proving to me, by authorities, that which at any moment I can bring to the test of experiment. . . . If discussing a difficult problem were like carrying a weight, since several horses will carry more sacks of corn than one alone will, I would agree that many reasoners avail more than one; but discoursing is like [running] and not like carrying, and one hunter by himself will run farther than a hundred drayhorses. When [a scientist] brings up such a multitude of authors, it does not seem to me that he in the least degree strengthens his own conclusions, but he ennobles the cause . . . of myself, by showing that we reason better than many men of established reputation. If [others] insist that I must believe [because ancient authors say so] . . . that the Babylonians cooked eggs by swiftly whirling them in a sling, I will believe it; I will believe it; but I must say that the cause of such an effect is very remote from that to which it is attributed, and to find the true cause I shall reason thus. If an effect does not follow with us which followed with others at another time, it is because, in our experiment, something is wanting which was the cause of the former success; and if only one thing is wanting to us, that one thing is the true cause. Now we have eggs, and slings, and strong men to whirl them, and yet they will not become cooked; nay, if they were hot at first, they more quickly become cold; and, since nothing is wanting to us but to be Babylonians, it follows that being Babylonians is the true cause why the eggs became cooked, and not the friction of the air, which is what I wish to prove. . . . I, at least, will not . . . blindly and blunderingly believe whatever I hear and barter the freedom of my intellect for slavery to one as liable to error as myself."

St. Peter's Basilica in Rome. The pope and other officials of the Catholic church opposed Galileo's writings and ideas.

Italian, however, Galileo bypassed the university professors, who would have been the only ones who could have read the book if it had been written in Latin. Galileo's works made science understandable to people who had never been exposed to it before. His works sparked a fire which engulfed the world and transformed it.

Because Galileo had made *Dialogue* accessible to everyone, religious leaders greatly feared that the book would mobilize people's thoughts against the church. Galileo's book encouraged people to think for themselves and discover the world through their own experiences. His book seemed to cry out for people to reject authority for its own sake. Political and church authorities were uneasy with a scientist who flaunted authority.

The clergy who oversaw the school system in Europe wanted the book squashed because it threatened the basis of everything they taught. If they lost control of the school system, they believed, they would lose authority over those noblemen, princes, and kings who held control of Eu-

rope. University scholars mobilized against Galileo's writing because they refused to admit they had given their lives blindly to the defense of false beliefs. Following the publication of *Dialogue*, Giovanni Ciampoili, a friend of Galileo's, wrote to him that "the Jesuits were much offended and preparing to strike back."[54]

Disobedience

Urban also turned against the book and its author. When *Dialogue* was published, the pope was facing enemies both within and outside of the church. Europe was enmeshed in political turmoil, and France was threatening the established powers of Austria, Italy, and Spain. To combat France, Urban had been forced into a secret alliance with the Swedish king, who was a known heretic. When the alliance was exposed, Urban alienated the church's traditional supporter, the emperor of Austria. It was rumored that the pope's enemies began plotting against him in Italy.

Pope Urban VIII made a secret alliance with the Swedish king, Gustavus Adolfus (above). When it was exposed, Urban lost much of his political control.

"The Pope lives in fear of poison," wrote one diplomatic correspondent. "He has . . . shut himself in; no one is admitted without being searched. The 10 miles of road are heavily patrolled. . . . The garrisons and lookouts on the coast have been reinforced."[55]

Urban saw Galileo's book as another threat to his power. He thought Galileo had made a fool of him by putting his speeches in the mouth of a character whose name, Simplicio, when literally translated meant "simpleton" or "fool." Urban did not like the fact that Galileo's book seemed to be testing the church's authority and calling out for freedom of thought. In 1632 Urban recalled the book and prohibited any more from being printed. But Urban's move came too late. The booksellers had none to return to the pope. Copies of the book had been purchased as quickly as they were printed. In addition, Galileo had already sent a copy to a friend in Germany who immediately began translating it into Latin for distribution throughout Europe.

The public especially resisted the pope's ban. Priests, monks, princes, and kings vied with each other to buy copies of

Because of his political unpopularity, Pope Urban VIII feared loss of power. Perceiving Galileo's book as a threat to his control, he tried to recall the published copies and prohibited future printings.

The Church's Growing Suspicion

The first official document showing the church's changing attitude toward Galileo can be seen in a letter sent in 1632 from Father Riccardi to the Inquisition in Florence, as excerpted from Ludovico Geymonat's book, Galileo Galilei.

"Signor Galilei's book has arrived in these parts, and there are many unsatisfactory things in it which the superiors wish adjusted at all costs. Therefore [the pope] orders (though only my name is to be used) that the book be withheld, and not leave that city without the necessary corrections being sent from here; nor shall the book be issued. Your Reverence may discuss this with the illustrious [pope] and proceeding gently, make sure that everything is done effectively."

Dialogue on the black market and to keep them out of the hands of members of the Inquisition who would have destroyed them. The price of the book rose from the original half *scudo* to four and six *scudi* (almost one hundred dollars) all over Italy. While the public worked to keep Galileo's book in circulation, his enemies were determined to destroy the book and its author.

In August Galileo received a note of warning from a friend in Rome, who said, "I have heard that they are having a commission of irate theologians to prohibit your *Dialogue;* and there is no one on it who understands mathematics. . . . I fear the violence of people who do not [understand]. . . . God keep you."[56]

Knowing that such a commission could result in a trial by the Inquisition, Galileo persuaded his patron, the grand duke of Tuscany, to send a message to the pope asking for an impartial commission. But the grand duke's message went unheeded. "Your Galileo," the pope responded, "has

ventured to meddle with things that he ought not and with the most grave and dangerous subjects that can be stirred up in these days."[57]

Following the pope's angry response, Galileo was convinced that he needed to defend *Dialogue* himself. He believed he could win the commission's support if he were allowed to present the book point by point to the commission. But his request was denied. The commission would rule on the book without talking to its author.

While Galileo and his friends were worried about the commission, many of his supporters were sure that it would clear Galileo. After all, the scientist had received permission to publish the book from the Inquisition, and the pope himself had written the introduction. The consensus of Galileo's friends was

There is nothing they can do to you. But things are out of hand for a while, because the pope has made an impulsive

Fear the Violence of People Who Do Not Know

Father Campanella's letter to Galileo in 1632 warns his friend of the growing movement against him. The letter is taken from Giorgio de Santillana's book, The Crime of Galileo.

"I have heard that they are having a commission of irate theologians to prohibit your *Dialogue;* and there is no one on it who understands mathematics or recondite things.

Please note that you may hold that the opinion of the moving Earth was properly forbidden, without having also to believe that the reasons alleged are good. This is a theological rule. . . . The decry is valid but not the motivation. . . .

I fear the violence of people who do not know. . . . My advice is, have the Grand Duke write that, as they have put Dominicans, Jesuits . . . and secular priests on the commission they should admit also Father Castelli and myself. . . . Or you may ask for us as lawyer and attorney in thy case; and, if we do not win it, hold me for [a fool]."

Father Campanella feared for Galileo's life.

move. Sit tight, do not yield more than you have to, but do not irritate them. They have gone off half-cocked, and now they feel they have to run the tilt; when they come back, it will be time to talk.[58]

The Summons

In the end, Galileo's fears proved true. The papal commission reported that Galileo had supported the Copernican system and that he had gained permission to print his book through trickery. These crimes were serious, and it was recommended that Galileo be brought to trial by the Inquisition. On September 23, 1632, a message from Rome arrived at the residence of Florentine Inquisitor Stefani. Written to Antonio Cardinal Barberini, the younger brother of the pope, it directed Stefani to instruct Galileo, under orders of the Holy Office, to travel to Rome as soon as possible to appear before the Inquisition.

In despair, Galileo wrote to Francesco Cardinal Barberini, Urban's nephew:

> This vexes me so much that it makes me curse the time devoted to these studies in which I [worked] and hoped to deviate somewhat from the beaten path generally pursued by learned men. I not only repent having given the world a portion of my writings, but feel inclined to suppress those still in hand, and give them all to the flames.[59]

Galileo begged Urban for a reprieve. He was close to seventy years old and he was in ill health. His doctors testified that the two-hundred-mile trip to Rome might kill him. But the pope was adamant. "He must come," Urban replied. "He can come by very easy stages, in a litter, with every comfort, but he really must be tried here in person." The Holy Office sent a mandate. If Galileo delayed any longer, a commission would be sent from Rome to escort him in chains. Galileo accepted the command saying,

> If neither my great age, nor my many bodily infirmities, nor the depth of my grief, nor the hazards of a journey in such a condition are considered sufficient reasons by this high and sacred tribunal, for granting a dispensation, or at least a delay, I will undertake the journey, esteeming obedience to be worth more than life.[60]

With these words Galileo told his accusers that he was a faithful and obedient member of the Catholic church and that he would follow the pope's orders, even if it cost him his life. In January 1633 Galileo set out for his last visit to Rome. By this time the scientist was so ill that he had to be carried the entire way in a litter.

Chapter

6 Galileo's Last Years

Galileo's trial was more than the prosecution of one man for his views: it was the collision of two different belief systems vying for dominance. By silencing Galileo the church was trying to hang on to its power as the supreme authority on all matters—both religious and scientific. It wanted to discourage new scientists from threatening traditional beliefs and encouraging people to question authority. Galileo foresaw that the church's power would decline as it refused to acknowledge scientific truths. He believed that the Bible was a moral authority but that it could not be used to understand science:

> I think that in the discussions of physical problems we ought to begin not from the authority of scriptural passages, but from sense-experiences and necessary demonstrations. . . . God [is not] any less revealed in Nature's actions than in the sacred statements of the Bible.[61]

Galileo defends his theories and writings before the Inquisition.

On the other hand, the religious, political, and intellectual leaders of Galileo's time had a lot invested in continuing a belief in ancient authorities and biblical verses. Galileo's enemies tried to dismiss his theories as a waste of time and a dangerous threat to authority. Pope Urban voiced this concern when he said, "It would be extravagant boldness for anyone to go about limit[ing] the Divine power and wisdom to some one particular conjecture of his own."[62]

The Trial

Galileo arrived in Rome on February 13, 1633, after twenty-three painful days on the road. He was allowed to rest at the home of the Tuscan ambassador to regain his strength before the trial. During his weeks there Galileo began to hear rumors of the charges against him. According to his friends in the church, the main charge against him was that he had tricked the church licensers into granting him permission to publish his book.

These charges were less serious than he expected, and Galileo was confident that he would be found innocent. Galileo wrote to his brother-in-law in Florence, "We hear at last that the many and serious accusations are reduced to one and the rest have been dropped. Of this one I shall have no difficulty getting rid, once the grounds of my defense have been heard."[63]

While Galileo was resting, the Inquisition worked to build a case against him. The Inquisition judges found themselves in a precarious position. The Catholic church had licensed *Dialogue,* the Inquisition had approved it, and the pope had

written an introduction to the book. To rule afterwards that everyone was wrong and the book contained heresy would put the church in an embarrassing position. But the pope had requested a verdict against the scientist, and Galileo's religious and scientific enemies were pushing the Inquisition to bring Galileo to trial. While searching the church archive, the Inquisition found an unsigned document from Cardinal Bellarmine to Galileo. This note would prove to be Galileo's downfall.

The first hearing against Galileo was convened on April 12, 1633, by Father Vincenzo Maculano of the Inquisition. Like all of those brought before the Inquisition, Galileo was not given a copy of the charges against him, nor was he allowed to have a lawyer defend him. Usually heretics were considered guilty until they could prove their innocence, and the accused were rarely able to succeed.

While Galileo feared the power of the Inquisition, he also felt confident that he had done nothing wrong. He had evidence to support this. But Galileo's confidence soon gave way to fear as the trial began. The first day was devoted to examining his visit to Rome in 1616 when he had met with Cardinal Bellarmine. Under questioning, Galileo recounted his meeting with Bellarmine:

The Lord Cardinal Bellarmine signified to me that the aforesaid opinion of Copernicus might be held as a conjecture, as it had been held by Copernicus, and his Eminence was aware that, like Copernicus, I only held that opinion as a conjecture, which is evident from [a letter Bellarmine wrote that states:] "It appears to me that . . . Signor Galileo acts wisely in contenting

Threatened with torture and death, Galileo renounces his ideas before the Inquisition.

[himself] with speaking [hypothetically] and not with certainty. . . . It means, in other words that opinion taken absolutely, must not be either held or defended."[64]

Galileo presented his signed statement from Bellarmine, which asserted that the Copernican theory could be discussed as one of many ideas.

The questioning continued all day before the Inquisition presented the cornerstone of its case—the unsigned document, which stated that Galileo, and Galileo alone, was prohibited from writing or teaching the Copernican theory in any way whatsoever. This, the Inquisitors claimed, was the document that Bellarmine had presented to Galileo in 1616. (Historians are not sure whether the document was a forgery or a draft that was considered and rejected.) Galileo had never seen the document. When it was presented at his trial, Galileo knew the church was going to denounce his book and prohibit the spread of his ideas. But, even though the paper was not signed by either

Bellarmine or Galileo, the Inquisition used it to condemn Galileo. The church claimed that Galileo had tricked the licenser and published his book even though he had been expressly forbidden to do so.

At the end of the day Galileo returned to the ambassador's house to await the Inquisition's judgment. By this time some of the judges had become uneasy with their task. Some visited Galileo and urged him to denounce his book. If only he would admit his guilt and ask for forgiveness, then the Inquisition would be more lenient with him, the judges cautioned. Cardinal Barberini wrote of his visit with Galileo:

> I suggested . . . that the Holy Congregation should grant me permission to [talk] with Galileo, in order to render him sensible of his error and bring him . . . to a confession. . . . I entered into discourse with Galileo yesterday afternoon, and after many arguments and rejoinders . . . I obtained my object, for I brought him to a full sense of his error, so that he clearly recognized

that he had erred and gone too far in his book. And to all this . . . [he seemed] willing to confess. . . . I trust that [the pope] will be satisfied that in this way the affair is being brought to such a point that it may soon be settled without difficulty. The court will maintain its reputation; it will be possible to deal leniently with the culprit; and whatever the decision arrived at, he will recognize the favor shown him.[65]

If Galileo refused to confess, the Inquisition would be forced to continue its questioning—and even use force and torture if necessary—the judges told him. From his time as a medical student, Galileo knew the pain the Inquisition could inflict. The idea of being stretched on the rack or burned to death was more than the elderly scientist could face. He agreed to confess his crime before the Inquisition and ask for forgiveness.

On April 30, 1633, Galileo was called before the Inquisition to make his confession. The elderly scientist knelt before the tribunal and renounced all that he believed to be true:

I Galileo . . . swear that I have always believed, do believe, and by God's help will in the future believe all that is held, preached, and taught by the Holy Catholic and Apostolic Church. But [after being ordered by the church] to altogether abandon the false opinion that the Sun is the center of the world and immovable and that the Earth is not the center of the world and moves and that I must not hold, defend, or teach in any way whatsoever verbally or in writing, the said false doctrine. . . . I wrote and printed a

Galileo kneels before the tribunal while he makes his confession.

book in which I discuss this new doctrine [which had] already [been] condemned. . . . I [now] abjure, curse, and detest [supporting the idea that is heresy] and generally every other error . . . contrary to the Holy Church.[66]

Galileo's friends thought that his confession would end the trial, and Galileo had been led to believe his punishment would be light. Some of his supporters thought that being forced to make the confession would be all the punishment the scientist would receive. But the Inquisition was under pressure to make an example of Galileo. In a statement following Galileo's

Galileo's Confession

A translation of the transcript of Galileo's confession before the Inquisition, taken from Ludovico Geymonat's book, Galileo Galilei, *follows.*

"I, Galileo Galilei, son of the late Vincenzo Galilei . . . aged seventy years, arraigned personally before this tribunal, and kneeling before you, most Eminent and Reverend Lord Cardinals, Inquisitors general against heretical depravity throughout the whole Christian Republic, having before my eyes and touching with my hands, the holy Gospels—swear that I have always believed, do now believe, and by God's help will for the future believe, all that is held, preached, and taught by the Holy Catholic and Apostolic Roman Church. But whereas—after an injunction had been judicially [told] to me by this Holy Office, to the effect that I must altogether abandon the false opinion that the sun is the centre of the world and immovable, and that the earth is not the centre of the world, and moves, and that I must not hold, defend, or teach in any way whatsoever, verbally or in writing, the said doctrine, and after it had been notified to me that the said doctrine was contrary to Holy Scripture—I wrote and printed a book in which I discuss this doctrine already condemned . . . without presenting any solution of [it]; and for this cause I have been pronounced by the Holy Office to be vehemently suspected of heresy, that is to say, of having held and believed that the sun is the centre of the world and immovable, and that the earth is not the centre and moves:

Therefore, desiring to remove from the minds of your Eminences, and of all faithful Christians, this strong suspicion, reasonably conceived against me, with sincere heart and unfeigned faith I abjure, curse, and detest the aforesaid errors and heresies, and generally every other error and set whatsoever contrary to the said Holy Church; and I swear that in the future I will never again say or assert, verbally or in writing, anything that might furnish occasion for similar suspicion regarding me; but that should I know any heretic, or person suspected of heresy, I will denounce them to this Holy Office."

confession, the Inquisition declared that Galileo had "incurred all the censures and penalties imposed" against heretics. Galileo was to be confined for the rest of his life to his small villa in Arcetri. He was to remain under strict house arrest and would not be allowed to see most of his family and friends. He was to publish nothing and was never again to discuss his theories. His ideas were banished from all of the schools and universities that once honored him. In all of the scientific writings where he had been referred to as "renowned," the Inquisition ordered the word changed to "notorious."

Legend has it that after hearing his sentence, Galileo whispered *"Eppur si muove"*—"The earth does move." Most historians, noting that such an act of defiance could have cost Galileo his life, doubt that the story is true.

The Aftermath

Galileo left the trial feeling bitter and broken. He found it hard to accept that he had been sentenced through trickery. His work was over, and the ideas he had fought so hard to prove were banished. Following the trial, he wrote to a friend:

> I do not hope for any relief, and that is because I have committed no crime. I might hope for and obtain pardon, if I had erred; for it is to faults that the prince can bring indulgence, whereas against one wrongfully sentenced while he was innocent . . . how clearly it would appear if some power would bring to light the slanders, frauds, stratagems, and trickeries that were . . . in Rome in order to deceive the

The Sentence

On June 22, 1633, the Inquisition pronounced the following sentence against Galileo. It is taken from Giorgio de Santillana's book, The Crime of Galileo.

"We say, pronounce, sentence and declare that you, Galileo, for the things found in the trial and confessed by you, have made yourself . . . vehemently suspected of heresy, namely to have held and believed false doctrine, contrary to the Holy and Divine Scriptures. . . . We are agreeable that you will be absolved provided that first, with sincere heart and unfeigned faith, you abjure, curse and detest the above mentioned errors and heresies. . . . We order that the book *The Dialogue* by Galileo Galilei be prohibited by public edict. We condemn you to formal prison . . . and we impose on you as salutary penances that for the next three years you say the seven penitential psalms once a week."

authorities! . . . It is left me only to succumb in silence under the flood of attacks, exposures, derision, and insult coming from all sides.[67]

Galileo knew that other scientists might become more cautious after his censure. He was correct. The scientific revolution in Italy ended. Following the trial, Galileo's greatest scientific contemporary, René Descartes, stopped publishing in France, a Catholic nation, and went to Sweden. The torch of the scientific revolution was extinguished in Italy.

Poet John Milton summed up the atmosphere following Galileo's imprisonment. He found that in Italy

where this kind of inquisition tyrannizes, I have sat among their learned

Poet John Milton (middle figure) visited Galileo during his imprisonment and bemoaned the lack of intellectual freedom in Italy.

men and been counted happy to be born in such a place of philosophic freedom as they supposed England was, while they themselves did nothing but bemoan the servile condition into which learning amongst them was brought; that this was it which had damped the glory of Italian wits, that nothing had been written now these many years but flattery.[68]

An Inquiring Mind

Although his sentence prevented him from pursuing Copernicus's ideas, Galileo did not stop delving into other scientific problems. During his years of enforced silence and solitude, Galileo wrote one of the greatest works of his life, *Discourses on Two New Sciences*. This was a monumental work that he had been thinking about for

After Galileo's trial, fellow scientist René Descartes stopped publishing his findings in France.

years. In it Galileo explored the field of physics. He answered many of the questions about motion and force, including how to calculate the speed at which bodies fall and the effects of friction on a moving object. Galileo first began to consider why and how things moved when he was a teenager. His first work on the topic was a small tract entitled *De Motu (On Motion)*, written in 1589 when he was twenty-five years old. At that point Galileo was still grappling with traditional ideas and the book sounds faintly Aristotelian. In the book he wrote that the motion of an object was controlled by its nature. He stated that heavy objects fall to the earth because it is their nature to be close to the center of the earth.

During the years Galileo continued to develop his ideas about motion and force. His new book would be the culmination of his life's work. But Galileo feared that *Discourses on Two New Sciences* would never be published, because the church had refused to let Galileo have any visitors at

DISCORSI
E
DIMOSTRAZIONI
MATEMATICHE,
intorno à due nuoue scienze

Attenenti alla

MECANICA & i MOVIMENTI LOCALI;

del Signor

GALILEO GALILEI LINCEO,

Filosofo e Matematico primario del Serenissimo
Grand Duca di Toscana.

Con vna Appendice del centro di grauità d'alcuni Solidi.

IN LEIDA,
Appresso gli Elsevirii. M. D. C. XXXVIII.

The title page of Galileo's Discourses on Two New Sciences, *which was published in Holland after one of Galileo's friends smuggled the manuscript out of Italy.*

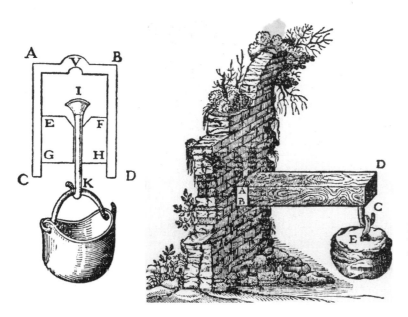

Illustrations from Galileo's Discourses on Two New Sciences *explaining (left) the creation of a vacuum and (right) the breaking point of a beam.*

Arcetri. But as Galileo got older and his health continued to fail, this restriction was eased slightly. His friend, Prince Mattia de' Medici, smuggled out Galileo's manuscript in 1638. It was ultimately printed in Holland, a Protestant country where the Catholic church had no power.

The church did not persecute him for this book for a number of reasons, the chief being that it could not prove Galileo had written it. Galileo claimed to have had nothing to do with the book's publication. To appease the Inquisition his friends stated that one of his admirers had taken the book and secretly sent it out of the country to be printed. For this reason the church could not accuse Galileo of violating his sentence. Also, the book was more technical than *Dialogue* and harder for people to understand. As historian Sebastian Timpanaro wrote, *"Two New Sciences* is a book no less Copernican than the *Dialogue Concerning the Two Chief World Systems.* Theologians did not condemn it because they did not understand it."[69]

Galileo's Physics

Discourses brings the three friends from *Dialogue* together once again and, like the earlier book, it is set up as a series of discussions over a period of days. In his foreword to *Discourses,* Galileo wrote:

> My purpose is to set forth a very new science dealing with a very ancient

---

A Letter Home

Galileo became resigned to his isolation, but he continued to miss his family. In a series of letters to Alessandra Bocchineri, the sister of his son Vincenzo's wife in 1641, Galileo hints at his loneliness and lingering bitterness toward the state. The following is taken from Ludovico Geymonat's book, Galileo Galilei.

"I can never tell you sufficiently the pleasure I should take in uninterrupted leisure to enjoy your conversation, elevated above usual feminine talk, so much so that little more significant and perceptive can be expected from the most experienced and practiced men in the world. I am sorry that your invitation [to visit] cannot be accepted, not only because of the many indispositions that oppress me in my old age, but because I am held in prison for reasons well known to my lord, your husband, the distinguished cavalier. . . . I have received your welcome letter at a time when it is a great consolation to me, and I have been confined to bed by serious illness for many weeks. My cordial thanks to you for the courteous affection that you show for my person, and for the condolence you send me in my miseries and misfortunes."

---

subject. There is, in nature, perhaps nothing older than motion, concerning which the books written by philosophers are neither few nor small; nevertheless I have discovered by experiment some properties of it which are worth knowing and which have not hitherto been either observed or demonstrated. Some superficial observations have been made. . . . So far as I know, no one has yet pointed out [the ideas explained in this book].[70]

Before publication of this book scientists tried to explain why motion happened. But Galileo was more interested in *how* it happened. Why did a rolling ball keep rolling after it was pushed, and why did it eventually stop rolling? To him these were the important questions.

Throughout the book Galileo states his ideas and then proves them through experiments. He wrote that every error and fallacy would easily be discovered and corrected if people tested their ideas through experiments. Galileo believed observation and experimentation was the only way scientists could learn about the world because it was impossible for experiments to lie.

Through his experiments Galileo discovered that the earth was a world full of movement. He theorized that once something started moving, it would continue to move unless something stopped it. In *Discourses* he wrote, "Any velocity once imparted to a moving body will be rigidly maintained as long as the external causes . . . of retardation are removed. . . . [This velocity] would carry the body at a uniform rate to infinity."[71] Now known as the First Law of Motion or the Law of Inertia, these motion discoveries laid the foundation for mathematical principles that formed the foundation of modern science.

Galileo continued his experiments until ill health and blindness forced him to stop in 1638. That year he wrote to a friend:

Alas . . . Galileo, your devoted friend and servant, has been a month totally and incurably blind; so that this heaven, this earth, this universe, which by my remarkable observations and clear demonstrations I have enlarged a hundred, nay, a thousand fold beyond the limits universally accepted by the learned men of all previous ages, are now shrivelled up for me into such a narrow compass [limited] by my own bodily sensations.[72]

In 1642, at the age of seventy-seven, Galileo died. The church still prohibited his writings from being published or studied and refused to let Galileo receive any honor, even after death. Galileo's body was buried in an unmarked grave, and many of his supporters feared that his discoveries would be forgotten. Instead, it would be the overwhelming power of the church that would slowly erode. Galileo's works would continue to light a fire of enthusiasm in others, who quickly took up where he left off.

7 Galileo's Legacy

Galileo died without seeing his ideas become widely accepted and other scientists carry on his work. In the centuries since his death Galileo's theories have been considered fundamental to modern science. To most scholars he is known as the father of the scientific revolution.

Scientific Method

Galileo's use of intense observation and experimentation is now an essential part of the training and practice of scientists. In little more than three hundred years, Galileo's method of developing a theory through observation and proving it through experimentation has become common practice.

Galileo discovered the property of pendulums, perfected the grinding of lenses, developed a theory of why the tides move, and destroyed the idea of an earth-centered universe. Each one of these achievements would have been enough to gain anyone a place in history. But Galileo, like Albert Einstein after him, believed that a unifying theory could explain all of nature. As he wrote in his book *Il Saggiatore (The Assayer),*

> Philosophy is written in that vast book which stands forever open before our

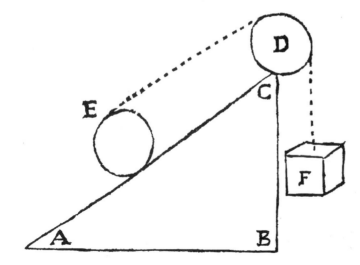

An illustration of one of Galileo's experiments to measure the force of a ball rolled down an incline. Galileo's methods of observation and experimentation have become accepted scientific procedure.

The title page of Galileo's book Il Saggiatore (The Assayer), *in which the scientist writes of his belief in a unifying rule of nature.*

eyes, I mean the universe; but it cannot be read until we have learnt the languages and become familiar with the characters in which it is written. It is written in mathematical language . . . without which it is humanly impossible to comprehend a single word.[73]

Through the Generations

Arousing an interest in science in others was one of Galileo's greatest talents. He made a major contribution to physics and to science as a whole through his role as a great teacher. Through his own writings, and the work of his students, Galileo's ideas eventually swept the world. Even though he could not change the minds of his critics during his life, Galileo was able to entice future generations with his books and experiments. Galileo's scientific ideas did not triumph by convincing his opponents, but rather because his opponents eventually died and a new generation grew up that was comfortable with his ideas. His pupils, and those who would come after, were Galileo's true legacy. Of them, he wrote: "What I consider more important, there have been [questions] opened up to this vast and most excellent science, of which my work is merely the beginning, ways and means by which other minds more acute than mine will explore its most remote corners."[74]

Francesco Redi used Galileo's methods of observation to disprove the theory of spontaneous creation.

Evangelista Torricelli experiments with a mercury-filled tube to observe the effects of atmospheric pressure.

Galileo's pupils included many great scientists, such as Father Benedetto Castelli, who made breakthroughs in the field of hydrodynamics; Alfonso Borelli, who used Galileo's theories in *The Assayer* to explain how volcanic eruptions were caused by the movement of thermal layers; Francesco Redi, who used Galileo's methods of observation in the field of biology to disprove spontaneous creation, the idea that insects spring to life. Galileo's illustrious students also included Evangelista Torricelli. One of Galileo's last students, Torricelli followed in his teacher's footsteps by taking

the post of mathematician to the grand duke of Tuscany. Torricelli discovered the principles of atmospheric pressure while experimenting with a mercury-filled tube. In 1657 he helped found the Accademia del Cimento and dedicated it to spreading Galileo's scientific method. During the ten years the academy operated, reports of its work spread throughout the scientific circles of Europe and helped broaden support for Galileo's method. Among other topics, members of the academy continued to work on Galileo's theory of motion and the use of the pendulum as a timekeeping device.

Galileo's work also inspired later scientists, such as Englishman Isaac Newton, who was born the year Galileo died. Newton used Galileo's writing to answer the remaining questions about motion—velocity, acceleration, force, and gravity.

Isaac Newton relied on Galileo's work to develop his theories of velocity, acceleration, force, and gravity.

Newton expanded on Galileo's work and developed the laws of motion and force, some of the basic principles of the universe. Newton and Galileo proved the laws of motion that remain accurate today, such as a body at rest tends to remain at rest unless acted upon by an outside force; and a body in motion tends to remain in motion unless acted on by an outside force.

Galileo's life and works continue to touch scientists. Albert Einstein wrote of him that the theme

which I recognize in Galileo's work is the passionate fight against any kind of dogma based on authority. Only experience and careful reflection are accepted by him as criteria for truth. Nowadays it is hard for us to grasp how sinister and revolutionary such an attitude appeared at Galileo's time, when merely to doubt the truth of opinions which had no basis but authority was considered a capital crime and punished accordingly . . . but in theory, [today] . . . the principle of unbiased thought has won out.[75]

Galileo's ideas have indeed triumphed through the centuries after his death. Everyone now accepts Galileo's ideas, even the church which once feared them so much. During the past thirty years the Catholic church has allowed the publication and reexamination of the documents used against Galileo. As the documents were studied, the possibility arose that the memorandum that was used to incriminate Galileo might have been faked. With this came the prospect that the judges

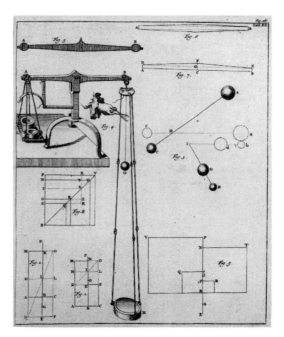

The design for one of Newton's experiments with gravity.

might have erred in condemning the Italian scientist. Pope John Paul II called for the formal exoneration of Galileo, and in 1982 the church absolved him. After more than three hundred years Galileo had won his argument with the church.

Galileo is remembered for his ability to break with authority and seek his own answers, his desire to share his knowledge with the world, his ability to present scientific information in a clear and enjoyable form, his commitment to truth and science, and his ability to inspire others. As future astronomers probe the heavens for new stellar bodies, or doctors search for the cure for cancer, they use Galileo's scientific method and follow in the path of the Italian scientist who proved the earth was a planet spinning in space.

Notes

Chapter 1: The Early Years

1. Laura Fermi and Gilberto Bernardini, *Galileo and the Scientific Revolution.* New York: Basic Books, 1961.

2. Colin Ronan, *Galileo.* New York: G.P. Putnam's Sons, 1974.

3. Fermi and Bernardini, *Galileo and the Scientific Revolution.*

4. Fermi and Bernardini, *Galileo and the Scientific Revolution.*

Chapter 2: Years of Discovery

5. Fermi and Bernardini, *Galileo and the Scientific Revolution.*

6. Fermi and Bernardini, *Galileo and the Scientific Revolution.*

7. Alan Smith, *Science and Society,* London: Harcourt Brace Jovanovich, 1972.

8. Giorgio de Santillana, *The Crime of Galileo.* New York: Time Inc., 1955.

9. Santillana, *The Crime of Galileo.*

10. Fermi and Bernardini, *Galileo and the Scientific Revolution.*

11. Stillman Drake, *Galileo Studies.* Ann Arbor, MI: The University of Michigan Press, 1970.

12. Ronan, *Galileo.*

13. Drake, *Galileo Studies.*

14. Fermi and Bernardini, *Galileo and the Scientific Revolution.*

15. Ronan, *Galileo.*

16. Galileo Galilei, Albert Van Helden, tr., in *The Sidereal Messenger.* Chicago: University of Chicago Press, 1989.

17. Ludovico Geymonat, *Galileo Galilei.* New York: McGraw-Hill Book Company, 1957.

18. Geymonat, *Galileo Galilei.*

19. Van Helden, tr., in *The Sidereal Messenger.*

20. Van Helden, tr., in *The Sidereal Messenger.*

21. Fermi and Bernardini, *Galileo and the Scientific Revolution.*

22. Santillana, *The Crime of Galileo.*

23. Santillana, *The Crime of Galileo.*

24. Santillana, *The Crime of Galileo.*

Chapter 3: A Rising Storm

25. Santillana, *The Crime of Galileo.*

26. Santillana, *The Crime of Galileo.*

27. Santillana, *The Crime of Galileo.*

28. Fermi and Bernardini, *Galileo and the Scientific Revolution.*

29. Charles E. Hummel, *The Galileo Connection.* Downers Grove, IL: InterVarsity Press, 1986.

30. Hummel, *The Galileo Connection.*

31. Santillana, *The Crime of Galileo.*

32. Geymonat, *Galileo Galilei.*

33. Santillana, *The Crime of Galileo.*

34. Santillana, *The Crime of Galileo.*

Chapter 4: Facing the Church's Wrath

35. Santillana, *The Crime of Galileo.*

36. Santillana, *The Crime of Galileo.*

37. Geymonat, *Galileo Galilei.*

38. Santillana, *The Crime of Galileo.*
39. Santillana, *The Crime of Galileo.*
40. Hummel, *The Galileo Connection.*
41. Geymonat, *Galileo Galilei.*
42. Geymonat, *Galileo Galilei.*
43. Geymonat, *Galileo Galilei.*
44. Geymonat, *Galileo Galilei.*
45. Geymonat, *Galileo Galilei.*
46. Geymonat, *Galileo Galilei.*
47. Geymonat, *Galileo Galilei.*

Chapter 5: Dialogue

48. Santillana, *The Crime of Galileo.*
49. Santillana, *The Crime of Galileo.*
50. Geymonat, *Galileo Galilei.*
51. Santillana, *The Crime of Galileo.*
52. Santillana, *The Crime of Galileo.*
53. Santillana, *The Crime of Galileo.*
54. Santillana, *The Crime of Galileo.*
55. Santillana, *The Crime of Galileo.*
56. Santillana, *The Crime of Galileo.*
57. Santillana, *The Crime of Galileo.*
58. Santillana, *The Crime of Galileo.*
59. Santillana, *The Crime of Galileo.*
60. Santillana, *The Crime of Galileo.*

Chapter 6: Galileo's Last Years

61. Fermi and Bernardini, *Galileo and the Scientific Revolution.*
62. Fermi and Bernardini, *Galileo and the Scientific Revolution.*
63. Santillana, *The Crime of Galileo.*
64. Geymonat, *Galileo Galilei.*
65. Santillana, *The Crime of Galileo.*
66. Geymonat, *Galileo Galilei.*
67. Santillana, *The Crime of Galileo.*
68. Santillana, *The Crime of Galileo.*
69. Geymonat, *Galileo Galilei.*
70. Fermi and Bernardini, *Galileo and the Scientific Revolution.*
71. Fermi and Bernardini, *Galileo and the Scientific Revolution.*
72. Jacob Bronowski, *The Ascent of Man.* Boston: Little, Brown and Company, 1973.

Chapter 7: Galileo's Legacy

73. Geymonat, *Galileo Galilei.*
74. Fermi and Bernardini, *Galileo and the Scientific Revolution.*
75. James Brophy and Henry Paolucci, *The Achievement of Galileo.* New York: Twayne Publishers, 1962.

For Further Reading

William Bixby, *The Universe of Galileo and Newton.* New York: American Heritage, 1964.

James Brophy and Henry Paolucci, *The Achievement of Galileo.* New York: Twayne Publishers, 1962.

Deborah Hitzeroth, *Telescopes: Searching the Heavens.* San Diego: Lucent Books, 1991.

Sidney Rosen, *Galileo and the Magic Numbers.* Little, Brown, and Company, 1958.

William Wallace, *Galileo and His Sources.* Princeton, NJ: Princeton University Press, 1984.

Richard Westfall, *Essays on the Trial of Galileo.* South Bend, IN: University of Notre Dame, 1990.

Works Consulted

Daniel J. Boorstin, *The Discoverers.* New York: Random House, 1983. World history with a focus on the discoveries that aided human progress.

Jacob Bronowski, *The Ascent of Man.* Boston: Little, Brown and Company, 1973. Scientific philosophy and history. Book outlines the development of humans with a focus on how scientific and technological changes impacted human development and made possible further developments.

A.C. Crombie, *Augustine to Galileo.* London: Falcon Educational Books, 1952. Traces the development of scientific thought from the beginning of the Dark Ages through the fifth century, the Renaissance, and seventeenth century.

Stillman Drake, *Galileo Studies.* Ann Arbor, MI: University of Michigan Press, 1970. Examines the works of Galileo as an outgrowth of Medieval science. Focuses on how the intellectual beliefs of his time influenced him.

Laura Fermi and Gilberto Bernardini, *Galileo and the Scientific Revolution.* New York: Basic Books, Inc., 1961. A biography that draws heavily from translations of Galileo's works and notes. Includes a complete translation of Galileo's work *The Little Balance.*

Galileo Galilei, Albert Van Helden, tr., *The Sidereal Messenger.* Chicago: The University of Chicago Press, 1989. A complete translation of Galileo's *Sidereus Nuncius.* Introduction and conclusion written by the translator places Galileo's work in the context of his society.

Ludovico Geymonat, *Galileo Galilei.* New York: McGraw-Hill Book Company, 1957. A biography focusing on Galileo's philosophy of science. Additional notes by historian Stillman Drake.

Karl Hufbauer, *Exploring the Sun: Solar Science Since Galileo.* Baltimore, MD: The Johns Hopkins University Press, 1991. Explores scientific achievements since Galileo. Part of the NASA history series.

Judy Jones and William Wilson, *An Incomplete Education.* New York: Ballantine, 1987. History of art, economics, philosophy, religion, and science.

Hugh F. Kearney, *Science and Change 1500–1700.* New York: McGraw-Hill Book Company, 1971. History of science and its impact on society.

Ernan McMullin, *Galileo, Man of Science.* New York: Basic Books, 1967. A compilation of papers presented on Galileo at the Galileo Quatrecentary Congress held at the University of Notre Dame in April 1964.

Edward Peters, *Inquisition.* New York: Free Press, 1988. History of the development of the Inquisition with focuses on the Inquisition's impact on art, literature, and science.

Pietro Redondi, *Galileo: Heretic.* Princeton, NJ: Princeton University Press, 1987. A presentation of new documents discovered in the Archives of the Vatican Holy Office. Author uses these documents to argue that the Jesuits had plotted Galileo's downfall because of his threat to church authority.

Colin Ronan, *Galileo*. New York: G.P. Putnam's Sons, 1974. Biography of Galileo includes extensive primary source quotes.

Giorgio de Santillana, *The Crime of Galileo*. New York: Time Inc., 1955. An examination of Galileo's works from the viewpoint of Galileo as a reformer. Author presents Galileo as a devout Catholic who is determined to bring the church into line with new scientific discoveries.

Nathan Spielberg and Bryon D. Anderson, *Seven Ideas That Shook the Universe*. New York: John Wiley & Sons, 1987. History which explores physics, mechanics, and astronomy.

Index

permission for, 59, 60
political problems of,
    65–66
supports Galileo, 57–58
printing press
    invention of, 9–10
Protestant church
    Martin Luther and, 21–22
    compared to Catholicism,
        22, 78
Ptolemy
    astronomical theories of,
        14
    Galileo rejects, 20, 28
    Galileo studies, 13
    Greater Astronomical Syntax,
        The, 14
pulsilogia, 16

Querengo, Antonio
    on Galileo's arguments, 53

Redi, Francesco
    biology experiments, 82
Renaissance, 9–10
    education during, 9, 12,
        15, 65
Riccardi, Father Nicolo
    editing of *Dialogue,* 60
Ricci, Ostilio
    tutors Galileo in mathemat-
        ics, 16–17

Sagredo, Giovanni, 61
    warns Galileo, 34, 35
St. Thomas Aquinas, 12–13
Salviati, Filippo, 61, 63
Saturn
    Galileo's observations of,
        37
Scheiner, Christopher
    study of sunspots, 45–46
science
    conflict with religion,
        40–41, 48, 49
scientific method
    Galileo uses observation
        and experimentation,
        7, 15–16, 57, 79, 80
scientific revolution, 7, 76
Simplicio, 61, 63, 66
    study of Greek and Roman
        philosophers, 12–13
Stefani, Father Giacinto
    approval for *Dialogue,* 61
    orders Galileo to trial, 69
sunspots
    Galileo's explanation of, 45
    Scheiner's explanation of,
        45

telescope
    controversy about, 31, 36
    invention of, 25–26, 33, 38

popularity of, 26–27
Timpanaro, Sebastian, 78
Torricelli, Evangelista
    atmospheric pressure
        experiments, 82

University of Padua
    Galileo and
        experiments at, 19–20
        life contract and, 26
        teaches mathematics, 18,
            20
University of Pisa
    Galileo and
        Chief Mathematician, 36
        studies at, 13–17
        teaches mathematics,
            17–18
        theories banned, 40, 75

Venus
    Galileo's observations of,
        37, 39
Vinta, Belisario, 35, 36
Visconti, Father Rafael
    editing of *Dialogue,* 60

Welser, Mark, 45
Wotton, Sir Henry, 30

Zarlino, Geoseffo, 11

Picture Credits

Cover photo by Library of Congress

Ann Ronan Picture Library, 31, 45 (bottom), 62, 73, 77 (bottom left & right), 83

Ann Ronan Picture Library and E. P. Goldschmidt & Co., Ltd., 80

Art Resource, 8, 20, 28 (top), 39 (top)

The Bettmann Archive, 10, 12, 13 (bottom left), 17, 25, 27, 41, 49, 52, 56, 57, 65, 66 (top), 70, 76 (top)

Historical Pictures/Stock Montage, 11, 19, 26 (bottom), 34, 36, 42, 51 (top), 53, 66 (bottom), 72, 77 (top), 81 (both)

Library of Congress, 7, 9, 13 (top & bottom right), 14 (both), 21, 22, 23, 40, 43, 44, 47, 61, 76 (bottom), 82 (bottom)

The Mansell Collection, 15 (both), 33, 59, 68, 82 (top)

NASA, 28 (bottom), 29, 37, 39 (bottom)

University of California/Lawrence Berkeley Laboratory, 26 (top)

UPI/Bettmann, 45 (top)

About the Authors

Deborah Hitzeroth and Sharon Heerboth are sisters who live in Texas. Ms. Hitzeroth's writing background includes a B.A. degree in journalism from the University of Missouri and four years of newspaper experience. She has worked as a section editor on a weekly paper and as a free-lance writer for magazines in New York and Fort Worth. This is her fourth book.

Ms. Heerboth has a B.S. degree from the University of Missouri and an A.A. degree from Texas State Technical Institute. Her writing background includes in-house technical and educational writing. This is her second book.